NEW DIRECTIONS FOR STUDENT SERVICES

Margaret J. Barr, *Northwestern University*
EDITOR-IN-CHIEF

M. Lee Upcraft, *The Pennsylvania State University*
ASSOCIATE EDITOR

# The Changing Role of Career Services

Jack R. Rayman
*The Pennsylvania State University*

EDITOR

D1527682

Number 62, Summer 1993

JOSSEY-BASS PUBLISHERS
San Francisco

THE CHANGING ROLE OF CAREER SERVICES
*Jack R. Rayman* (ed.)
New Directions for Student Services, no. 62
*Margaret J. Barr,* Editor-in-Chief
*M. Lee Upcraft,* Associate Editor

Microfilm copies of issues and articles are available in 16mm and 35mm,
as well as microfiche in 105mm, through University Microfilms Inc., 300
North Zeeb Road, Ann Arbor, Michigan 48106.

LC 85-644751          ISSN 0164-7970          ISBN 1-55542-699-9

NEW DIRECTIONS FOR STUDENT SERVICES is part of The Jossey-Bass
Higher and Adult Education Series and is published quarterly by Jossey-
Bass Inc., Publishers, 350 Sansome Street, San Francisco, California
94104-1310 (publication number USPS 449-070). Second-class postage
paid at San Francisco, California, and at additional mailing offices. POST-
MASTER: Send address changes to New Directions for Student Services,
Jossey-Bass Inc., Publishers, 350 Sansome Street, San Francisco, California
94104-1310.

SUBSCRIPTIONS for 1993 cost $45.00 for individuals and $60.00 for institutions, agencies, and libraries.

EDITORIAL CORRESPONDENCE should be sent to the Editor-in-Chief,
Margaret J. Barr, 633 Clark Street, 2-219, Evanston, Illinois 60208-1103.

Cover photograph by Wernher Krutein/PHOTOVAULT © 1990.

# CONTENTS

EDITOR'S NOTES     1
*Jack R. Rayman*

1. Contemporary Career Services: Theory Defines Practice     3
*Jack R. Rayman*
This chapter provides an introduction to the forces that have thus far shaped the environment of career centers in the 1990s. It then outlines a career development paradigm based on extant career development theory and specifies the individual programs and services that such a paradigm suggests for the contemporary career center.

2. The Organization and Impact of Career Programs and Services Within Higher Education     23
*David S. Bechtel*
Absent a traditional organizing theme or practitioner consensus on philosophy, purpose, or professional practice, the organization of career services and programs within academic settings is so varied and diffuse that it represents a continuum of arrangements and assignments rather than a generally accepted operational pattern.

3. Placement Services     37
*Richard A. Stewart*
This chapter describes the important elements of a comprehensive placement service and discusses a range of practical issues currently confronted by the placement profession.

4. Career Counseling: A Call to Action     57
*Mary J. Heppner, Joseph A. Johnston*
This chapter presents eight themes that constitute both a springboard for careful evaluation of current career counseling practices and a call to action for the career counseling profession.

5. Career Programming in a Contemporary Context     79
*Jean M. Yerian*
This chapter discusses issues ranging from needs assessment and programming for the majority, to programming for special populations and topics, to program evaluation. It also touches on experiential learning programs. Included are over one hundred programming ideas from the author's 1992 national survey of career center directors and an appendix of contact information on their programs.

6.  Concluding Remarks and Career Services Imperatives      101
for the 1990s
*Jack R. Rayman*
Themes common to all of the chapters in this volume are summarized, and ten
imperatives for career centers in the 1990s are presented.


INDEX                                                       109

# EDITOR'S NOTES

The college placement office has evolved from a single-purpose administrative unit offering a narrow range of placement services to a comprehensive services center providing a complex array of career services to multiple constituent groups. While career development and placement centers vary in size, mission, and organizational structure, the trend is inescapably toward greater size, increasing centralization, and a broader, more comprehensive mission. Indeed, to reflect these changes, most placement offices have changed their names to Career Development and Placement Services, Career Planning and Placement Services, or Career Services.

Unfortunately, in many institutions the title change has signaled little change in actual function. In some cases, career development and placement services continue as single-purpose on-campus recruiting operations with the emphasis narrowly focused on getting the right student in the right room at the right time with the right employer, that is, placement as a point-in-time event. In other cases, career centers have extended their array of services backward in time to include career development and planning programs for freshmen and sophomores (and even prospective students), and forward to include programs of career assistance and involvement for alumni throughout the life span, while at the same time broadening their services to meet the needs of an increasingly diverse student body, that is, career development as a lifelong process.

The purpose of this volume, *The Changing Role of Career Services,* is to examine the changing role of career centers on college and university campuses, to identify current issues confronting the profession, and to suggest practical means of addressing those issues in the 1990s. In Chapter One, I provide an overview of the economic and social forces that have thus far shaped the environment of college and university career centers in the 1990s. I then describe a down-to-earth career development paradigm based on extant career development theory and specify the individual programs and services that such a paradigm suggests for the contemporary career center.

In Chapter Two, David S. Bechtel explores the position of career services within the college and university setting: How should career services be organized and configured? Should career services be an academic function or a student services function? What are the historical forces that have shaped the organization and administration of career services? How critical are career services to the mission of an institution of higher education, and what are the emerging administrative and organizational trends?

In Chapter Three, Richard A. Stewart focuses on the placement function. He explores the ongoing redefinition of the term *placement,* identifies key placement services, and discusses current issues associated with each. He concludes that the keys to surviving and prospering in the 1990s are the intelligent application of technology, a redoubling of our commitment to personalized customer service, and an increased commitment to advocacy on behalf of career services vis-à-vis the institutional power structure.

In Chapter Four, Mary J. Heppner and Joseph A. Johnston focus on career counseling. They present eight themes that constitute both a springboard for careful evaluation of current career counseling practices and a call to action for the career counseling profession. They conclude that self-examination and change will be necessary if career counselors are to meet the challenges of the 1990s.

In Chapter Five, Jean M. Yerian focuses on career programming and acknowledges the vital role that programming plays in the success of today's comprehensive career services center. She discusses issues ranging from needs assessment and programming for the majority, to programming for special populations, to program evaluation. She also shares over one hundred programming ideas from her national survey of career center directors and provides an appendix of contact information on their programs.

Finally, in Chapter Six, I attempt to identify issue-oriented threads that are woven through all five chapters despite their separate foci. I take those threads and reweave them into a set of career center imperatives for the 1990s.

It is my hope that career counseling practitioners will find this volume to be a useful resource: as a stimulus in addressing current issues, as an ally in advocating for additional resources or improved organizational or administrative structures, and as a source of reassurance that the profession not only will survive the 1990s but also will emerge from the decade stronger and nearer the core of campus life.

Jack R. Rayman
Editor

*JACK R. RAYMAN is director of career development and placement services and affiliate professor of counseling psychology and education at The Pennsylvania State University, University Park.*

*This chapter provides an introduction to the forces that have thus far shaped the environment of college and university career centers in the 1990s. It then outlines a career development paradigm based on extant career development theory and specifies the individual programs and services that such a paradigm suggests for the contemporary career center.*

# Contemporary Career Services: Theory Defines Practice

*Jack R. Rayman*

In the mid 1980s, college and university career centers were in their heyday. Fueled by the new-found optimism of the Reagan administration, together with the enormous increases in defense spending that accompanied the Strategic Defense Initiative, the American economy was supercharged. Demand for entry-level professional employees in the fields of engineering, science, and business was running at all-time high levels. Fortune 500 companies eagerly sought out entry-level talent on college campuses from coast to coast. This high demand for college graduates was of the type that "traditional" college and university placement offices were nearly perfectly suited to serve. In the academic years 1988–1989 and 1989–1990, most placement offices conducted record numbers of on-campus interviews (Pennsylvania State University, 1990). In the euphoria of the hour, career centers were adding staff; and the focus at most centers, which had begun to shift to career development, counseling, and planning in the early 1980s, returned to the job placement function. In a way, what was happening in career centers paralleled what had happened to the economy and society in general: There was a certain giddiness and a return to the "old way" of doing things. It was the last gasp of a failed "supply-side" mentality, and it worked—for a few years. As business boomed, for the first time in recent memory demand for business majors on some campuses outstripped that for engineers and scientists. Students flocked to the business curriculum, perceiving it as an easy path to high salaries and the accompanying yuppie lifestyle. With demand so high, it is little wonder that career centers temporarily refocused much of their attention on job placement and relaxed the slow but steady evolution that had been taking place from a job placement emphasis in the 1950s and 1960s to a career planning and counseling emphasis in the 1970s and 1980s (Casella, 1990). Then reality set in.

## Current Socioeconomic Influences on College and University Career Centers

A host of circumstances, economic and social, converged to refocus and reshape the goals and objectives of the career center of the 1990s.

**The Economic Boom Goes Bust.** On-campus recruitment has always been sensitive to economic ups and downs, but the recession of the 1990s has been a white-collar recession unlike the blue-collar recession of the late 1970s (*Cam Report*, 1992b). The environment thus created is one of intense competition between the recently laid-off college-educated employee with five to ten years of solid work experience and the current graduate. On-campus recruitment plummeted by as much as 50 percent on many campuses between 1989 and 1992 (American Association of Engineering Societies, 1992; Commission on Professionals in Science and Technology, 1992). Increasingly, very qualified current graduates now find themselves in direct competition with experienced professionals for entry-level jobs. This situation has created a heightened anxiety for current students and recent graduates, an anxiety that permeates the college campus and especially the career center. With on-campus recruiting activity at its lowest level in twenty years, career centers must refocus their energy on helping students "take the job search to the employer." While demand for on-campus interviewing facilities continues to decline, the demand for outreach programs, seminars, workshops, and career planning and counseling services has reached an all-time high.

**Restructuring of Business and Industry and Increasing Global Competition.** Never before have business and industry been so competitive. Most large businesses find that they simply cannot compete in the world market and continue to carry the enormous overhead represented by a huge bureaucracy of middle and upper management—the euphemism most often heard as a solution is "rightsizing." The reality is that most Fortune 500 companies are downsizing, big time. They are flattening their organizations, stripping away layers of management, becoming "lean and mean" (*Cam Report*, 1992a). This work force reduction has led to the elimination of many white-collar positions and created an army of unemployed, highly qualified, relatively young, experienced professionals and middle managers who are now competing directly with current college graduates for jobs. The impact on career centers has been a greatly increased demand for alumni career services, a practical manifestation of the much theorized "lifelong process nature" of career development.

**Structural Shift from a Manufacturing-Based to a Service-Based Economy.** In 1920, 46 percent of non–farm wage and nonsalary employment in the U.S. economy was in the goods-producing sector and 54 percent was in the service-producing sector; by 1990, the goods-producing sector had been reduced to 23 percent while the service sector expanded to 77 percent (Ottinger, 1992). Manufacturing jobs have always been higher paying than comparable positions in the service sector of the economy. As more and more manufacturing facilities have moved offshore, the number of high-paying jobs associated with manufacturing has diminished substantially (U.S. Department of Labor, 1991a). This trend means that the college graduates of the 1990s are being forced to accept relatively lower-paying jobs than their predecessors. Few things in life are as stressful and anxiety provoking as being asked to adjust one's career expectations downward in this way. The prospect of selling vacuum cleaners door-to-door is not high on the list of career aspirations for most college graduates, no matter what their majors. Dealing with student distress and concern over this increasing disparity between their sometimes fancifully high career aspirations and their realistic job options has become a major item on career center agendas in the 1990s. Programming designed to assist students as they make the transition from college to work has taken on new importance. Early emphasis on career planning and "career choice reality therapy" for college freshmen and sophomores has become essential, and the once separate enterprises of academic advising and career development are becoming increasingly intertwined.

**End of the Cold War and Its Impact on Huge Defense Contractors.** Many of the very largest employers of college graduates (for example, General Electric, Chrysler, and General Dynamics) have always depended heavily on defense contracts. As these defense contracts dry up, the once highly profitable defense industry finds itself in a depression. While the full impact of the end of the Cold War on the general economy will not be known for some time, the immediate impact on key defense-related industries such as the aerospace industry has been significant (U.S. Department of Labor, 1991a). The resulting turbulence and uncertainty about future job possibilities has caused heightened anxiety for technical students as they seek to predict (guess) which majors will be in demand when they graduate. At the same time, the downsizing of the military complex will dump significant numbers of technically trained employees into the job market, further exacerbating an already highly competitive situation.

**Small Companies and Organizations as Sources of Economic Growth in the 1990s.** Unfortunately, most small companies and organizations have not traditionally looked to colleges and universities as sources of entry-level employees (*Cam Report*, 1992a). Many have primitive or underdeveloped human resources departments, and few actively recruit college graduates. None has a history of close relationships with college and university career centers. The task of providing for the efficient flow of college-educated employees to these emerging small employers has already proved to be a formidable challenge for career centers. (It is much easier to manage on-campus recruiting for five large companies, each conducting one hundred student job interviews, than it is to manage the activity of one hundred small companies, each conducting five student job interviews.) In the helter-skelter world of emerging small companies, employer development is taking on a whole new meaning. Career centers will have to develop new techniques and strategies to help students access this new, less accessible (hidden) job market.

**Changing Nature of Professional and Scientific Employment in the U.S. Economy.** It was once the case that college graduates who went to work for "Ma Bell" (AT&T), "Big Blue" (IBM), and many others of the Fortune 500 could count on careers with those corporations until retirement. Many of the major corporations had what was referred to as a "full-employment" policy, which meant in effect that no one was ever laid off. Rather, the corporation took significant responsibility for the long-term career development of its employees. That era is gone. Increasingly, corporations are contracting professional and technical expertise with a view toward cutting personnel and benefit costs. Concepts that have been utilized for years in fulfilling short-term clerical demands are now being applied to professional and technical employees. "Just-in-time" hiring and "staff leasing" are becoming commonplace at all levels of corporate America, and this trend places ever greater pressure and responsibility on the individual employee to manage his or her own career (*Cam Report,* 1992a). This necessity for the individual employee to assume responsibility for personal career development places greater demands than ever before on the staff of the career center (and the undergraduate curriculum) to equip college graduates with quality career development coping skills.

**Increased Debt Burden of Many Students.** Over the course of the last decade U.S. college students have acquired an ever-increasing debt load. It is not uncommon for a college student to be $20 thousand to $40 thousand in debt upon graduation. This increasing debt places enormous pressure on students to make career decisions based more on immediate job opportunities and high starting salaries than on the sounder, longer-term criteria of personal values, aptitudes, and interests. The pressure of debt often becomes a deterrent to quality career planning, development, and choice and exacerbates the already difficult task of career counseling.

**Increasing Diversity of the Student Body.** The changing nature of the student body mirrors that described in the *Workforce 2000 Executive Summary* (U.S. Department of Labor, 1987). Services and treatments that were once the mainstay of the career center are no longer sufficient to meet the increasingly diverse needs of the student body. Many minority students are first-generation college students. They have limited knowledge and experience dealing with the professional job search subculture and often need different, if not additional, career development assistance. Similarly, the task of providing for the career development and placement needs of returning adult students, disabled students, and other special populations will continue to be a challenge to career centers throughout the 1990s.

**Era of Severe Fiscal Constraints Within Higher Education.** Colleges and universities, which have long seemed immune from the vagaries of the economy, are now in the grip of a serious financial crisis. Many have implemented hiring freezes, most have developed creative early-retirement plans, and some have actually begun to issue pink slips. Because career centers are usually regarded as units of student services (and therefore are not a part of the core mission of the academy), they have become and will continue to be targets for staff and resource reductions at the very time that other economic and social forces suggest that career services should be expanded (Cage, 1992). This resource strain will almost certainly usher in a new era of fees-for-career-services in the 1990s.

Fiscal constraints have also caused many development offices to lean heavily on career centers in support of the development function. The long-standing relationship that career centers have maintained with corporate America is often seen by development office staff as a resource to be exploited for the purpose of securing gifts and grants. This trend is likely to continue in the 1990s.

It is within this context that the modern-day career center must operate. While many of these contextual constraints are born of current economic and social conditions, the fundamental core services must have their roots in a sound theoretical paradigm. One such paradigm is the main subject of this chapter.

## Theoretical Paradigm for the Career Center

When most students, faculty, and families hear the office title Career Development and Placement Services or Career Center, they think of that office as a place where students go (or are referred) in the final semester of their senior year when it becomes apparent that they are going to suffer the indignity of having to work for a living. Indeed, the most visible service offered by career development and placement centers is usually job placement, and, more specifically, on-campus interviews conducted by the placement service. This unfortunate perception has its roots in an obsolete conception of career development and in a history of single-purpose placement offices designed principally to meet the job search needs of engineering and business students.

In fact, placement is only a very small part of what goes on in a modern-day office of career development and placement services. As student needs have changed and as the general public has become increasingly aware that a career is not simply a job but rather a sequence of jobs held over the course of a lifetime, placement offices have changed both their names and their functions (College Placement Council, 1991). Indeed, some modern comprehensive career development and placement services devote up to 60 percent of professional staff time to the functions of counseling and programming, while the remaining 40 percent is spent assisting students with the task of finding their initial job, or what is commonly known as placement (Pennsylvania State University, 1991). This reality requires a new understanding of the term *career development*. What is it really? Why is it important? And which configuration of services is necessary to facilitate career development in institutions of higher education?

## Definition of Career Development

In my judgment, career development is a critically important component of human development—a process that takes place from approximately age four until death. Perhaps it has been most aptly described by Super (1963), who has characterized it as a sequence of life stages with attendant tasks and coping behaviors. The process nature of career development is analogous to physical development: A set of skills must be learned and a degree of mastery achieved before one can proceed to the next stage of development. Deficiencies in one stage of development can limit or restrict development in a subsequent stage; and although there are a normal or average rate and time by which most individuals reach each stage, there is also a wide range of individual differences. Although, historically, many different theorists have attempted to describe the career development process (Bordin, Nachmann, and Segal, 1963; Dudley and Tiedeman, 1977; Ginzberg, Ginsburg, Axelrad, and Herma, 1951; Holland, 1992; Krumboltz, 1979; Parsons, 1909; Roe, 1956; Super, 1957), contemporary critics have countered that extant career development theories are not appropriate for women, minorities, and other special populations (H. Astin, 1984; Fitzgerald and Crites, 1980; Gottfredson, 1981; Neff, 1968). However, Super's (1963) developmental theory still seems to have the most explanatory power and relevance to modern-day career development and placement services, and it is the most readily understood.

Figure 1.1 is an adapted version of Super's career development life-span model. In this schematic, chronological age appears in column 1. Column 2 shows the relationship of developmental stages to age, and column 3 consists of the developmental tasks identified by Super and the relationship of these tasks to ages and stages. Finally, the narrative portion of the schematic lists the coping behaviors associated with the tasks. Careful examination of this schematic clearly indicates that the "four critical years" (A. Astin, 1977) during which students are engaged in undergraduate education are critical not only because of their impact on beliefs, attitudes, and knowledge, as Alexander Astin has suggested, but also because of their impact on and relationship to career development. The crucial exploration stage, with its attendant tasks of crystallization, specification, and implementation, is

## Figure 1.1.  Model of Developmental Stages, Tasks, and Coping Behaviors

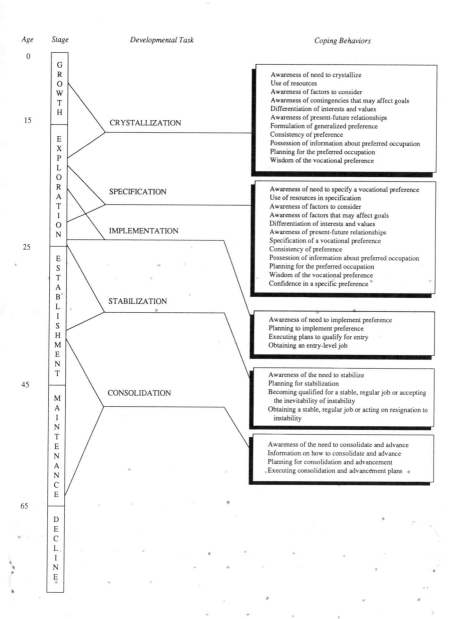

| Age | Stage | Developmental Task | Coping Behaviors |

*Source:* Adapted from Super, 1963.

clearly where much of the intense "action" is through the lifelong span of the career development process. The tasks themselves and facilitation of the attendant coping behaviors are the business of the modern-day career center.

## Importance of Career Development

It is curious that the literature of psychology—the science of human behavior—contains so little information on the "theater" (to use Super's [1957] term) where most humans spend up to one-half of their waking hours behaving: at work. While industrial and organizational psychology address some career development issues, much of this branch of psychology has to do with organizing and motivating workers to maximize productivity, with little emphasis on helping individual employees to maximize their job satisfaction and sense of well-being through personal career development. Indeed, it is fascinating that the general public's perception of psychology is that it consists of the business of diagnosing and treating mental illness, with a focus on abnormal behavior rather than on the expansive human enterprise of work or career behavior.

How important is career development? If one asks a group of one hundred people the simple question, "Who are you?" approximately 95 percent will respond in terms of what they do for a living. They will say, "I'm a teacher," "I'm a secretary," "I'm an engineer," or "I'm a . . . ." In other words, most people define who they are in terms of their occupations. As Super (1957) has put it, "The choice of a career is the implementation of a self-concept." That is, we define ourselves and our roles within society when we make career choices. When an individual chooses to go to medical school, she is expressing how she wants to relate to others. She is defining the terms of her relationships across a broad array of interactions with, for example, her patients, her colleagues, her relatives, the general public, the workplace. A career choice defines one's life-style, leisure activities, socioeconomic level, status, friends, and even enemies to a considerable degree!

Another indication of the importance of career development is that to the extent individuals enjoy "mental health," they are usually successful and satisfied careerwise. I do not propose any cause-effect relationship here, but the correlation that exists suggests that quality career development and mental health go hand in hand.

The fact that most individuals hold from five to fifteen different jobs or positions throughout the course of their career life further emphasizes that a career is not a point-in-time event but rather a lifelong process. Schlossberg (1984) has suggested that the critical points of career development are "transition points," including the transition between jobs. The effectiveness with which individuals deal with these transitions—from education to training, from training to employment, from one job to another, from work to retirement—determines in considerable measure their degree of career success and satisfaction. Individuals who have developed the facility to move from one identity and job to another with efficiency have mastered career development.

The point here is that career development is important. Indeed, it is far too important to leave to chance, and yet an alarming percentage of the population makes career choices by default. It does not have to be that way. College students can exercise a remarkable degree of control over their career destiny, but they must be willing to take responsibility for themselves. And that is where modern-day career development and placement services fit into the equation. The often-used quote, "Give a man a fish and he'll eat for today, but teach him how to fish and he'll eat for a lifetime" seems appropriate (though the language is now regarded as sexist!). It is not the primary goal of modern-day career development and placement services staff to get students jobs. It is their goal to teach young people the skills that they will need not only to get their first job and successfully make the transition from college to the world of work but also to skillfully and efficiently make subsequent transitions from job to job throughout the course of their life in an increasingly complex and rapidly changing economy and society.

That goal sounds great, but what does it mean and how can the practitioner translate high-sounding philosophy into a set of services that meet students' career development needs?

## A Career Development Paradigm

Figure 1.2 is a graphic depiction of a career development paradigm that draws from trait/factor, developmental, and decision-making career theory. The elements of the paradigm, their interactions, and the implications of the paradigm for college and university career centers are described in the accompanying narrative.

**Self-Knowledge.** The first element of career development is "Know thyself." It was good advice for the ancient Greeks, and it remains the fundamental building block of successful career development. But what elements or dimensions of self must an individual know or understand? The first of these are values. And, for our purposes, I define a value as a belief held so strongly that it guides one's actions. Psychologists have determined that there are between nine and twelve career-related values. Different terms are used to describe these different values, but nearly every researcher comes out with a list similar to the following, utilized in System for Interactive Guidance Information (SIGI) (Chapman, Norris, and Katz, 1973): high income, helping others, independence, interests, leadership, security, leisure, prestige, variety, and early entry.

Life is a valuing game. We define our values for all to see by the ways in which we use our time. Time is really all that any of us has to give, and the ways in which we use that time are strong indications of what we value most.

# Figure 1.2. Career Development Paradigm

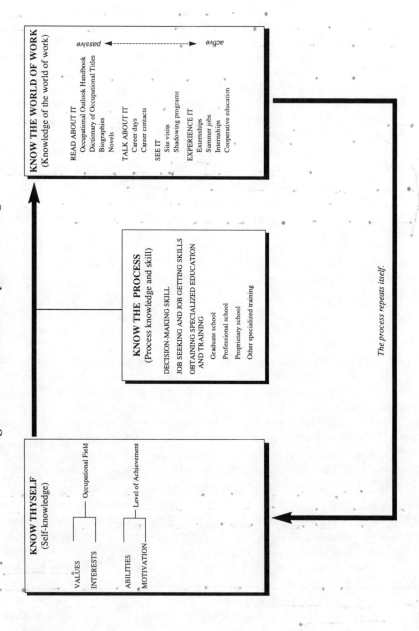

**KNOW THYSELF**
(Self-knowledge)

VALUES
INTERESTS — Occupational Field

ABILITIES
MOTIVATION — Level of Achievement

**KNOW THE PROCESS**
(Process knowledge and skill)

DECISION-MAKING SKILL
JOB SEEKING AND JOB GETTING SKILLS
OBTAINING SPECIALIZED EDUCATION
AND TRAINING
  Graduate school
  Professional school
  Proprietary school
  Other specialized training

**KNOW THE WORLD OF WORK**
(Knowledge of the world of work)

active ◄ - - - - - - ► passive

READ ABOUT IT
  Occupational Outlook Handbook
  Dictionary of Occupational Titles
  Biographies
  Novels

TALK ABOUT IT
  Career days
  Career contacts

SEE IT
  Site visits
  Shadowing programs

EXPERIENCE IT
  Externships
  Summer jobs
  Internships
  Cooperative education

*The process repeats itself.*

Sometimes students say, "What I really value is academic prowess." But then when we ask them, "What did you do last night?" they say, "I partied until 2 A.M." As in this example, we may pay lip service to a set of values, but our true values are those that guide our actions and use of time. The point here is that there are introjected values and internalized, or "real," values. Introjected values are those that we inherit from our parents, guardians, and other influential adults, but our real values are those that have been tested by reality and internalized. Clearly, values are a major determinant of career choice. The occupational field that a person ultimately chooses will be determined largely by the particular constellation of work values that the person holds and their relationship to one another. Because of the importance of values to the career development process, any career counseling session or career development system must devote substantial time and energy to values clarification.

But values are not the only personal characteristics or elements of self-knowledge that one must understand to achieve successful career development and choice. Another important element of self-knowledge is one's interests. There is considerable evidence to suggest that interests are a strong correlate of career and job satisfaction. Common sense suggests that if we are interested in something, we are more likely to enjoy being involved in it and thus to achieve greater satisfaction. For years, the Strong Interest Inventory, the Kuder Preference Inventory, the Self-Directed Search, and other interest inventories have been key tools utilized by career counselors to help clients better match their interests to those of various occupational groups. Clearly, interests are an important determinant of occupational field. Together, values and interests are the two categories of personal characteristics that most determine the occupational field in which an individual is likely to end up, but there are two other categories of personal characteristics that are also important to self-understanding.

The first of these is general ability. In the professional literature, general ability has been variously known as "general cognitive ability," "general mental ability," "general intelligence," "intelligence," or "IQ" (Gottfredson, 1988). Most individuals who have been admitted to a college or university have a relatively high level of general ability; nevertheless, an individual's general ability tends to be a determinant of his or her level of achievement within an occupational field and, more precisely, serves as a limiting factor. While the primary self-knowledge focus of career counseling and career development programming in colleges and universities is not on general ability, considerable effort must be spent helping students to better understand how able they are relative to their peers and determining the impact that ability will have on their career aspirations and success. In many ways, the fact that most college students are "multipotential" (in terms of general ability) complicates rather than simplifies the career decision-making process.

Finally, motivation is a major determinant of level of achievement within an occupational field. Persons who have tremendous drive, energy, and motivation to accomplish something can overcome deficiencies in general ability and other personal deficiencies to achieve at levels well beyond expectations. Often a skilled counselor can help a student develop a personal understanding of just how driven he or she is with a view toward facilitating realistic career choices and development.

These four types of personal characteristics—values, interests, ability, and motivation—are the key aspects of self that a college student must come to understand to ensure high-quality career development. Many educators would say that an understanding of self in terms of these dimensions is really the primary purpose of the undergraduate curriculum. Indeed, a reasonable goal for the undergraduate curriculum might be sufficient self-understanding to provide a sense of direction and purpose in life. Whether or not we consider this level of self-understanding to be the primary goal of an undergraduate education, the development of self-understanding along these four dimensions has become the primary content (or curriculum) of most individual career counseling sessions and many of the group sessions, seminars, workshops, and career courses conducted by the staff of the modern-day career center.

**Knowledge of the World of Work.** An understanding of who we are in terms of our values, interests, abilities, and motivation is not enough, and that brings us to the other half of the paradigm, knowledge of the world of work. Besides knowing who we are and what we want from life, we also have to have an understanding of what is available. Unfortunately, most students do not realize that there are more than twenty-two thousand different jobs available within U.S. society (U.S. Department of Labor, 1991b). In fact, the typical student knows very little about more than two or three jobs within this vast pool. A surprising number do not even know what their parents do for a living. As a society, we do a poor job of providing students with exposure to the thousands of different job possibilities that exist within our economy (although we probably do it better than just about any other society in the history of the world).

If we look at predictors of career choice, we find that socioeconomic class as represented by parental attainment continues to play a significant role (Hotchkiss and Borow, 1984). Thus, for example, one of the best predictors of whether or not a student will become a medical doctor is still whether or not one of his or her parents is a medical doctor. The same is true in a range of other occupations. In fact, there is a considerable caste structure still in existence in our society with respect to occupational choice and attainment. The major obstacle to more broad consideration of occupational options is often lack of exposure. Just as most people are prone to marry a neighborhood man or woman rather than someone from afar among the other five billion people on the face of the earth because they know their neighbors, many young people choose the occupation of a parent or close friend simply because they know so little about the more than twenty-two thousand other occupations among which they might choose. Thus, a key component of any career development and placement service is the provision of timely, accurate information about the occupational opportunities that exist within society. This is no small task. Securing timely information is difficult and expensive, massaging that information into a format and delivery system that students find attractive is even more challenging, and motivating students to access and interact with the information in a meaningful way is next to impossible.

The challenge of helping students develop a solid understanding of the world of work—how the world of work is organized, what occupations are available, what academic preparation and training are necessary, what life-styles are possible, and so on—falls to the career development and placement center. The compelling need for quality career information to support the career development process dictates that the modern career center provide the following forms of information access: dictionaries and encyclopedias of careers, actual position descriptions, trade publications, career biographies, books that accurately portray careers (for example, Studs Terkel's *Working*), career filmstrips and videotapes, computerized career information systems, career contact programs by telephone, alumni fellow programs, career fairs, plant visits, externship programs, relevant summer jobs, internship programs, and cooperative education programs.

Note that these different career information delivery systems have been listed along a continuum from those that can be accessed passively to those that require interaction and active participation. It has been my experience that passively delivered career information is usually a stimulus for users' profound and deep sleep! Interactive and participative delivery systems, while more effective, still do not ensure users' interest or understanding. The fact that there is so much career information available and that most students find it so deadly boring presents a daunting challenge. Most students are simply not willing to invest even a few hours in researching what they will be doing eight hours a day, five days a week, for the next forty years. At the same time, they are willing to invest countless hours in researching the purchase of a stereo, a new car, or a new appliance or securing a date for the weekend or a ticket to a concert or athletic event. This fundamental reality separates the approach that the U.S. Department of Labor has always taken to the provision of career information from the approach that is necessary for the successful modern-day career center: It is simply not sufficient to secure accurate and timely career information and make it available to students. In addition, we must somehow motivate the students to interact with the information, process the information, and draw on the information in support of career decision making and career implementation.

To summarize, it is not good enough to help students better understand themselves along the dimensions described on the left-hand side of Figure 1.2. Self-knowledge and understanding are necessary but not sufficient to ensure successful career development. Similarly, it is not good enough to simply provide students with access to high-quality, accurate, and timely career information. The two sides of the career development paradigm must be held together, and this is accomplished by process knowledge.

**Process Knowledge and Skill.** Process knowledge and skill are essential ingredients that allow the student to utilize self-knowledge and knowledge of the world of work and propel him or her from the exploration stage to the establishment stage of career development.

*Decision-Making Skill.* A common view of decision making is that anyone can make decisions if he or she has timely, accurate information. The reality is that many people do not know how to make effective decisions even though timely and accurate information is readily available. Further, we now know that people employ many different kinds of decision-making strategies (Gelatt, Varenhorst, and Carey, 1972), some of which are inappropriate for critical decisions such as career choices that have the potential to affect the remaining forty to sixty years of one's life. For example, some persons are "paralytic deciders," that is, they simply become paralyzed when confronted with the need to make a decision and end up allowing the environment to make the decision for them (not to decide is to decide!). Other people are "impulsive deciders," that is, they make decisions based on trivial, sometimes irrelevant information, often on the spur of the moment. Still others are "delaying deciders," that is, they delay repeatedly and only make the decision when there is no other option. In general, it seems clear that important decisions such as those that affect career development ought to be made through a rational decision-making process. Quality career counseling necessarily involves the teaching of decision making. Coaching or assistance with career decision making is a critical component of the career counseling process. Indeed, Tiedeman and O'Hara (1963) and Katz (1966) character-ized career development as a decision-making paradigm.

*Job Seeking and Job Getting Skills.* Still another element of process knowledge is the acquisition of job seeking and job getting skills. Many people do not realize that the best jobs are frequently not held by the best and most qualified people. Rather, the best jobs are frequently held by those people who have the most highly developed job seeking and job getting skills. Succinctly put, besides knowing one's strengths and weaknesses, and know-ing what kinds of career opportunities exist, one must also know how to market oneself effectively. The world is full of dissatisfied, overqualified, and underemployed individuals who for a variety of reasons refuse to accept the fact that the job search process is a marketing task, that a résumé is a million-dollar personal Super Bowl commercial, and that "you don't get a second chance to make a first impression." Clearly, résumé preparation, interview skill building, networking, assertion training, time management, and effective letter writing are critical elements of process knowledge that complete the career development equation. While excellent self-help is available on this subject from Bolles (1992), Figler (1988), Jackson (1991), Powell (1981), and countless others, the career center must still be the major purveyor of this process knowledge through seminars, workshops, and individual and group career counseling sessions.

*Obtaining Specialized Education and Training.* For college students, it is often the case that the career decision-making process leads to the realization that additional education and training are necessary. The students are then confronted with another obstacle-laden process to negotiate if successful career development is to be achieved. This process of application and admission to graduate, professional, and proprietary schools becomes yet another course in the curriculum of the career center.

## Career Development Paradigm Summary

As illustrated in Figure 1.2, career development consists of securing adequate self-information in terms of values, interests, abilities, and motivation. This process of developing self-knowledge is the essence of the undergraduate curriculum, but it is also an essential aspect of the curriculum of the modern-day career center and comprises much of the work of the career counseling enterprise in its many forms. Moreover, the provision of accurate, timely, career information is required via a multiplicity of delivery systems that range from reading about it in the career information center (the most passive) to experiencing it through an internship, a summer job, or cooperative education (the most involving). These two forms of knowledge (knowledge of self and knowledge of the world of work) then become the raw materials for the decision-making process (often assisted by counseling), which in turn leads to the need to develop quality job seeking and job getting skills (assisted by placement advising), which may also involve further education and training. The process culminates in the acquisition of an entry-level job.

## The Process Repeats Itself

Installation in an entry-level job often leads to the question "Isn't there more to life than this?" The individual then begins to reevaluate or reinventory his or her personal values, interests, abilities, and so on, and to cast about for additional information about other occupations that might provide a better fit for changing personal needs. These cycles may be repeated over the course of time. Over the life span, the process may be visualized as a sequence of cycles through the career development paradigm, each spiraling upward to higher levels of job success, satisfaction, and personal fulfillment. To facilitate progress through these recurrent cycles, career centers are increasingly being asked to develop an array of supportive alumni career services.

## Services Dictated by the Career Development Paradigm

College and university students clearly need assistance with the career development process. The career development paradigm delineated here calls for a comprehensive array of career services to enhance the career development effects of the college curriculum. The annotated outline in Exhibit 1.1 provides brief descriptions of the seven core functions of a comprehensive career service. I have chosen this format in the interest of saving space and providing the reader with a readily scannable listing of essential services. Not every college or university can provide all of these services. For that reason, the individual services described within each of the seven core functions appear in their approximate order of importance to successful discharging of the function. In other words, career centers that are able to deliver all of the individual services are more likely to be successful. Those that are not able to provide all of the services ought to at least provide those near the top of each list.

### Exhibit 1.1. Annotated Outline of Comprehensive Career Center Services

*Career Planning and Counseling Function*
Intake counseling: brief counseling available on a drop-in basis, with an emphasis on diagnosis and referral to the appropriate service or services
Individual career counseling: comprehensive career counseling delivered in the traditional one-on-one mode, with a limit of ten sessions per student
Career planning workshops and seminars: regularly scheduled programs to assist students with the career planning process
Assessment: comprehensive assessment services, including the assessment of interests, aptitudes, values, personality, and so on in support of career counseling
Computer-assisted career counseling: any of the computer-assisted career guidance systems (for example, DISCOVER or SIGI PLUS), available by appointment or on a walk-in basis
Group career counseling: the opportunity for students to participate in group career sessions organized around current topics and issues such as choosing a major, assertion training, and transitions from college to work
Courses for credit: courses offered through academic colleges or departments in which students receive systematic exposure to the career planning process for credit
Alumni life and career planning workshops: workshops marketed and implemented in a fashion similar to the job search workshops suggested below under the placement function

*Placement Function*
Placement advising: brief one-on-one assistance with résumé preparation, job search strategies, interview assistance, salary negotiations, and other placement-related issues
Training and skill development seminars and workshops: interview skills, job search strategies, résumé preparation, summer job search workshops, internship search workshops, and other topics as the need requires

Placement library: organized files of corporate and other employer literature (written materials, videotapes, and computer disks) to help students research potential employers

Job listing services: organized files or computerized files of company or organization position listings to which students may respond by telephone or letter

Career days and job fairs: on-campus events to provide students with exposure to various potential employers and provide employers with a means of identifying potential employees

On-campus recruiting: an efficient system that brings companies and other employers to campus for the purpose of conducting initial interviews for full-time employment as well as cooperative education and internship positions

Educational and graduate and professional school credential service: a system that allows students and alumni to maintain a permanent credential file for use in securing employment in the education sector or to secure admission to graduate or professional school

Résumé referral service: computerized résumé matching service to assist both alumni and employers

Alumni job search workshops: structured all-day job search workshops advertised by direct mail and held in geographical locations near large concentrations of alumni

*Career Programming Function*

Outreach programs and seminars: a range of outreach programs and seminars on topics dictated by user needs assessment and sponsored by the center

Special topics workshops and seminars: in response to special requests by faculty, student clubs, organizations, professional fraternities, and residence groups

Clearinghouse for requests and assignment of staff to conduct outreach programs

Minority programs: minority career fairs or career awareness days, special initiatives to ensure the appropriateness of services to minority students and other special populations, and outreach initiatives to ensure that special populations utilize career services in proportion to their numbers

Maintenance of an array of resources in support of outreach programming: videotapes, overhead transparencies, training materials, books, periodicals, and so on

Evaluation and support of all programs: systematic and ongoing evaluation of individual programs and presenters with a view toward continual improvement of both

Experiential education program coordination: cooperative education or formally structured, alternating work/education programs, usually in the technical fields of engineering, computer science, and so on; internship programs or less-structured, one-time work experiences sponsored by academic departments such as journalism, accounting, public administration, and social work; and externship programs (one-week shadowing experiences, usually with alumni)

*Information Support Function*

Placement library: see placement function services

Career information center: comprehensive career resources in support of counseling, placement, and programming functions but also for direct student use

Office handouts: an array of carefully conceived office handouts on such topics as résumé preparation, interviewing, job search strategies, secondary interviews, employment with the federal government, and transition from college to work

Follow-up surveys: direct-mail follow-up surveys of all graduates at all degree levels to determine placement rate, starting salaries, position title and description, and so on

Student advisory board: an advisory board made up of students from all critical constituent academic groups

## Exhibit 1.1. (continued)

Suggestion box: to be moved from one service location to another to constantly solicit customer feedback

Employer advisory board: a board of key employers to provide advice and feedback regarding all career services

Salary survey: ongoing salary surveys to keep abreast of current entry-level salary ranges by employer type and by academic discipline

### Communications Function

Office brochures: to describe office services to prospective student users

Placement manual: to describe placement services and provide essential placement information to all graduating seniors

Annual report: to provide both qualitative and quantitative descriptions of the year's accomplishments to faculty, staff, administration, and employers

Monthly informational newsletters: developed by a staff information specialist to keep career services staff and faculty abreast of current labor market trends and other career-related issues

Topical office handouts: on topics as described above under the information support function

Electronic message board: electronic sign located in the career center but accessible by students twenty-four hours a day, seven days a week, to deliver office announcements

Career newsletter: an office newspaper distributed with the college or university student newspaper to convey essential career center news to students and faculty

Electronic bulletin board: means of conveying career center information directly to students via the institutionwide electronic mail system

College newspaper to students: advertisements of events sponsored by the career center as well as an outlet for career center news releases

Radio spots: on campus or local radio to advertise career center services as well as promote specific events

Television spots: used in much the same way as radio spots

### Training Function

Work-study: provide training and work opportunities for work-study students

Volunteers: train and utilize local volunteers as well as alumni to assist in the delivery of career services

Undergraduate interns: train and utilize undergraduate interns to promote and assist in the delivery of career services

Graduate interns: provide graduate internships to key academic departments such as counselor education, counseling psychology, and student personnel administration

Practicum students: train and supervise graduate students in the delivery of career services in cooperation with key academic departments such as clinical psychology, counseling psychology, industrial and organizational psychology, and sociology

Graduate assistants: train, supervise, and utilize graduate students in the delivery of career services

Sponsored research: provide opportunities for doctoral and master's degree students to conduct research on topics related to the career development and choice process

### Assessment and Research Function

Annual postgraduation follow-up studies: conduct an annual follow-up study of all graduates at all degree levels (see placement function)

Conduct and publish periodic evaluations of individual services: employer services, counseling, placement, programming, and efficacy studies of career interventions

## Conclusion

The career services described above may be provided by staff, faculty, graduate students, volunteers, work-study students, or any combination of these groups. They may be delivered through centralized or decentralized systems among colleges or departments; they may be integrated with the curriculum or made optionally available; they may be delivered cooperatively with other student service agencies; and they may be delivered accidentally or intentionally. Whatever the means or mode of delivery, whatever the prevailing social or economic conditions, career development theory is the foundation on which a core of career services must be based. It has been the purpose of this chapter to make explicit this relationship between career development theory, student career development needs, and the services required to meet those needs. The chapters that follow focus on current issues and practice in the broad areas of career center organization and administration, placement services, career counseling services, and career programming.

## References

American Association of Engineering Societies. *Engineering Manpower Bulletin*, Nov. 1992.

Astin, A. W. *Four Critical Years: Effects of College on Beliefs, Attitudes, and Knowledge.* San Francisco: Jossey-Bass, 1977.

Astin, H. "The Meaning of Work in Women's Lives: A Sociopsychological Model of Career Choice and Work Behavior." *Counseling Psychologist*, 1984, *12* (4), 117–126.

Bolles, R. N. *The Nineteen Ninety-Two What Color is Your Parachute? A Practical Manual for Job Hunters and Career Changers.* Berkeley, Calif.: Ten Speed Press, 1992.

Bordin, E. S., Nachmann, B., and Segal, S. J. "An Articulated Framework for Vocational Development." *Journal of Counseling Psychology*, 1963, *10*, 107–116.

Cage, M. C. "To Shield Academic Programs from Cuts, Many Colleges Pare Student Services." *Chronicle of Higher Education*, Nov. 1992, pp. A25–A26.

*Cam Report.* 1992a, *15* (16), pp. 1–2.

*Cam Report.* 1992b, *15* (17), p. 2.

Casella, D. A. "Career Networking—the Newest Career Center Paradigm." *Journal of Career Planning and Employment*, 1990, *50* (4), 32–39.

Chapman, W., Norris, L., and Katz, M. *SIGI: Report of a Pilot Study Under Field Conditions.* Princeton, N.J.: Educational Testing Service, 1973.

College Placement Council. *1991 Career Planning and Placement Survey.* Bethlehem, Pa.: College Placement Council, 1991.

Commission on Professionals in Science and Technology. *Manpower Comments*, 1992, *29* (6), 3–6.

Dudley, G. A., and Tiedeman, D. V. *Career Development: Exploration and Commitment.* Muncie, Ind.: Accelerated Development, 1977.

Figler, H. E. *The Complete Job-Search Handbook: All the Skills You Need to Get Any Job and Have a Good Time Doing It.* Troy, Mo.: Holt, Rinehart & Winston, 1988.

Fitzgerald, L. S., and Crites, J. O. "Toward a Career Psychology of Women: What Do We Know? What Do We Need to Know?" *Journal of Counseling Psychology*, 1980, *27*, 44–62.

Gelatt, H. B., Varenhorst, B., and Carey, R. *Deciding.* New York: College Entrance Examination Board, 1972.

Ginzberg, E., Ginsburg, S. W., Axelrad, S., and Herma, J. *Occupational Choice.* New York: Columbia University Press, 1951.

Gottfredson, L. S. "Circumscription and Compromise: A Developmental Theory of Occupational Aspirations." *Journal of Counseling Psychology Monographs,* 1981, *28,* 545–579.

Gottfredson, L. S. "Reconsidering Fairness: A Matter of Social and Ethical Priorities." *Journal of Vocational Behavior,* 1988, *33,* 293–319.

Holland, J. L. *Making Vocational Choices: A Theory of Vocational Personalities and Work Environments.* (2nd ed.) Odessa, Fla.: Psychological Assessment Resources, 1992.

Hotchkiss, L., and Borrow, H. "Sociological Perspectives on Career Choice and Attainment." In D. Brown, L. Brooks, and Associates, *Career Choice and Development: Applying Contemporary Theories to Practice.* San Francisco: Jossey-Bass, 1984.

Jackson, T. *Guerrilla Tactics in the New Job Market.* New York: Bantam Books, 1991.

Katz, M. R. "A Model of Guidance for Career Decision Making." *Vocational Guidance Quarterly,* 1966, *15,* 2–10.

Krumboltz, J. D. "A Social Learning Theory of Career Decision Making." In D. H. Mitchell, G. B. Jones, and J. D. Krumboltz (eds.), *Social Learning and Career Decision Making.* Cranston, R.I.: Carroll Press, 1979.

Neff, W. S. *Work and Human Behavior.* New York: Atherton, 1968.

Ottinger, C. "What is the Service Sector?" *Research Briefs* (Division of Policy Analysis and Research, American Council on Education), 1992, *3* (4), pp. 1–12.

Parsons, F. *Choosing a Vocation.* Boston: Houghton Mifflin, 1909.

Pennsylvania State University. *Career Development and Placement Services Annual Report, 1989–90.* University Park: Pennsylvania State University, 1990.

Pennsylvania State University. *Career Development and Placement Services Annual Report, 1990–91.* University Park: Pennsylvania State University, 1991.

Powell, C. R. *Career Planning Today.* Bloomington, Ind.: Career Communications, 1981.

Roe, A. *The Psychology of Occupations.* New York: Wiley, 1956.

Schlossberg, N.K.C. *Counseling Adults in Transition: Linking Practice with Theory.* New York: Springer, 1984.

Super, D. E. *The Psychology of Careers.* New York: HarperCollins, 1957.

Super, D. E. "Vocational Development in Adolescence and Early Adulthood: Tasks and Behaviors." In D. E. Super, R. Starishevsky, N. Matlin, and J. P. Jordaan, *Career Development: Self-Concept Theory.* Research Monograph No. 4. New York: College Entrance Examination Board, 1963.

Tiedeman, D. V., and O'Hara, R. P. *Career Development: Choice and Adjustment.* New York: College Entrance Examination Board, 1963.

U.S. Department of Labor. *Workforce 2000 Executive Summary.* Washington, D.C.: Government Printing Office, 1987.

U.S. Department of Labor. Bureau of Labor Statistics. *Occupational Outlook Quarterly: Fall 1991.* Washington, D.C.: Government Printing Office, 1991a.

U.S. Department of Labor. Employment and Training Administration. Employment Service. *Dictionary of Occupational Titles.* (4th Ed.) Washington, D.C.: Government Printing Office, 1991b.

JACK R. RAYMAN *is director of career development and placement services and affiliate professor of counseling psychology and education at The Pennsylvania State University, University Park.*

*Absent a traditional organizing theme or practitioner consensus on philosophy, purpose, or practice, the organization of career services and programs within academic settings is so varied and diffuse that it represents a continuum of arrangements and assignments rather than a generally accepted operational pattern.*

# The Organization and Impact of Career Programs and Services Within Higher Education

*David S. Bechtel*

Practitioners of career assistance components at colleges or universities are often viewed by their institution as simple administrators performing a task, rather than as professionals with common philosophical and operation bases. Indeed, the orientation of some practitioners conforms to this view, while other practitioners struggle to defend and promote a professional developmental point of view. Lack of unanimity and the multifaceted orientation of practitioners have resulted in each college and university organizing career services and programs according to local and institutionally specific traditions and exigencies.

The organizational form, or combination of forms, adopted at a college or university depends on a number of factors: historical and traditional roles of career assistance units and their separate identity at the specific institution; professional affiliation and identity of career practitioners, generally and within the host institution; presence and importance of professional schools and academic units with strong ties to corresponding employment arenas; size and character of higher education institutions and, specifically, the host institution; and the institution's perspective on the importance and contribution of career services to the central purposes of the college or university. The organization and impact of career assistance efforts can best be understood in the context of history and tradition. This chapter presents references and source citations that may appear dated. They are offered to convey the prevailing thought of a time period and illustrate the evolution of career programs and services toward their present and future incarnations.

NEW DIRECTIONS FOR STUDENT SERVICES, no. 62, Summer 1993   © Jossey-Bass Publishers

OBSERVATION 1. *Career programs and services are difficult to describe and classify because there are multiple providers and each has its own history and orientation.*

Career programs and services do not fit neatly into the higher education setting or the organizational arrangements of colleges and universities. Unlike financial aid, they do not possess a mandated responsibility dictated by states, nor do they follow a uniformly accepted form of delivery such as found in admissions or records offices. Career services and programs serve a multitude of functions, and "career planning and placement personnel do not operate from a common philosophical, theoretical or definitional basis" (Scott, 1983, p. 13).

The College Placement Council (CPC) regularly surveys career offices at its member institutions (for example, CPC, 1991) soliciting the status of current organizational relationships and characteristics, but the definitive study on the organization of career services was conducted by Gary Scott at Northern Illinois University under the sponsorship of the CPC Foundation. In his report, *The Career Planning and Placement Office: Implications for the Future,* Scott (1983, pp. 13, 21, 33) made the following observations: "With respect to terminology common to the field, it is evident that a number of definitions exist for basic terms." "There is still a lack of unanimity of purpose among placement personnel." "Substantial differences in operating programs exist." "Few campuses were found to have all career development and placement services reporting to the same person or even the same division of the institution."

The task of describing career programs and services is aptly characterized by the metaphor of the elephant described by blind men. Holding onto the trunk, one blind man describes the animal as similar to a snake. Holding onto a leg, another blind man describes the elephant as resembling a tree. Career components can only be described by compiling the specific perspectives and descriptions of all that are involved in the diverse offerings and functions of career services.

**Placement Offices.** Mueller (1961, p. 481) describes the placement office in task completion terms as a service that involves "interviewing candidates, appraising, filing, duplicating and dispensing their credentials." He added a public relation component to the description by relating the role of placement to "exploring and creating opportunities in the outside world, as well as promoting confidence and rapport between candidate and employer, between the college and its public" (Mueller, 1961, p. 481).

*Career Counseling and Placement in Higher Education* (CPC, 1970) reflected the need for counseling, individual assistance, and a more organized approach to the job search process for college graduates. Most college placement offices subsequently broadened their involvement with students and now provide a wider variety of programs, activities, and personal contact.

Placement offices are thus less frequently named "placement." The 1991 CPC survey listed only 43 percent with "placement" included in the full office title, compared to 77 percent in the 1975 survey (CPC, 1991). The names of the offices have changed and services have been extended, but the focus and expertise of present placement office activity retain a task and public relations orientation to assist the job search process of college graduates and, in many cases, are not significantly different from their 1960s description.

**Counseling Offices.** As psychologist Edward Gordin (1949, pp. 120–121) observed, "Somehow I find it neither credible nor fruitful to conceive of individuals as having vocational problems which are not at the same time personal problems or vice versa." His was the prevailing view for the next several decades, and vocational counseling was part and parcel of assistance to students in pursuing education goals and completing their undergraduate degrees. However, Hoppock (1963, p. 111) observed that "what we now have in vocational counseling is far too many psychologists who regard placement as a dirty word, and any direct contact with the employment market degrading." This observation was echoed by Ginn (1979).

Career counseling, a new incarnation of vocational counseling, evolved to combine the work of the career planning and placement officer with that of the vocational psychologist (Ginn, 1979), as counseling offices addressed more immediate and life-threatening concerns. Career counseling's evolution has been in response to students' needs and the sophistication and expertise required for effective service, which are generally not part of the vocational counselor's repertoire. A broader and more comprehensive approach was demanded by students, faculty, alumni, and employers (Johnson and Figler, 1984).

**Minority Student Services.** Higher education recruited students in the 1970s who had previously been unable to attend college. Residential, academic, financial, and personal concerns of minority students were served by a central office on virtually every college campus in America. General career information is needed by all students, but other needs are most frequently related to subpopulations of students, such as the need to expand career horizons for women and minorities (Scott, 1983). The addition of career advising and programming to minority student service functions was considered sound educational policy in response to students' developmental needs (Miles, 1984).

**Preprofessional Advising.** Faculty mentors and faculty advisers have existed since the beginning of higher education (Stephens, 1970). Academic departments whose graduates, in the main, went on to professional schools such as law, medicine, or dentistry recognized the complexity of the professional school admissions process and also the value of an organized advising or assistance effort to help students gain acceptance into professional schools. The collection of letters of recommendation and advice on the selection of appropriate preparatory coursework were offered in consort with information about professional school admissions requirements. Preprofessional advising's faculty and academic roots, by and large, keep it distinct from other types of career assistance, but it performs an administrative and public relations role similar to that of placement offices.

**Cooperative Education and Internship Programs.** Cooperative education and internship programs, like preprofessional advising, originated in academic departments. The classic definition of an internship is an academically parallel out-of-classroom experience for academic credit. Placement offices, concurrently, helped students obtain summer employment with the companies and organizations with whom they maintained working relationships. The current, generally accepted definition now includes out-of-class, during-the-school-year, and summer work, and for-credit and not-for-credit, salaried and volunteer experiences. Programs vary in size, scope, and affiliation: sometimes with an academic department, sometimes with a placement office, and sometimes with a specifically designated office. The 1991 CPC survey reported that 63 percent of the respondents were involved in cooperative education or internship programs, whereas only 26 percent of the 1975 survey respondents offered these programs (CPC, 1991).

**Other Career Programs and Services.** Half of Scott's (1983) respondents indicated that other units on their campus were also involved in some form of career planning and placement. They listed academic departments and colleges; counseling centers; alumni offices; financial aid, minority affairs, and student employment offices; adult and women's resource centers; and campus libraries.

OBSERVATION 2. *Career assistance practitioners come from a variety of professional backgrounds, are attached to a variety of units, and identify with one or more of a variety of professional orientations and associations.*

Career assistance practitioners, because of the variety of career-related units, may identify with student affairs or academic campus units, faculty in a parent academic unit, an off-campus public with whom they relate operationally, or an off-campus group or association that performs similar functions and embraces a similar philosophy at other institutions of higher education. For example, premedical advisers may affiliate with premedical advisers nationally, with their respective academic disciplines such as the life sciences, or with the professional school admissions deans with whom they interact. Further, the National Association of Advisers for the Health Professions is one vehicle for professional affiliation and identity. Campus premedical advisers are thus drawn to others doing similar work on other campuses, or back to their own academic departments, or functionally to the admissions deans who accept their students. They are, because of the multiple foci of their attention, often unaware and unfamiliar with other career assistance practitioners, even on their own campus. Similarly, career planning and placement officers affiliate vertically with America's largest employers, with whom they too relate operationally. Practitioners are just doing their job as they see it for their students and for the segments of society that those students will enter (professional schools, Fortune 500 companies, or Big Six accounting firms) to meet the needs of immediate constituents as well as of society (Scott, 1983).

However defined and described, the various career assistance functions all stem from counseling, placement, academic units, and student services components; thus, practitioners come from diverse educational and experiential backgrounds (Scott, 1983). The practitioners of a particular career function may identify with their professional training or else the offices with which they are presently affiliated. Placement-oriented career practitioners may identify and affiliate with CPC, regional associations, the Association for School, College, and University Staffing (educational placement), the National Association for Law Placement, or one of the collegial groups within these associations. Counseling offices' career counselors may identify with the American College Personnel Association, the American Association for Counseling and Development, or, in some cases, the American Psychological Association. Cooperative education practitioners may relate to the Cooperative Education Association or the National Society for Internships and Experiential Education. Academic advisers who also do career counseling may affiliate with the Academic Affairs Administrators, and prehealth professional advisers have their own association, the National Association of the Advisers for the Health Professions. Faculty members' involvement in career assistance seems to strengthen their original faculty affiliations. They maintain close associations with their disciplines and the myriad of professional associations and societies of academia. Stephens (1971, p. 207) counseled placement and career counseling practitioners alike, "The diverse backgrounds of workers are often a barrier to communication and understanding and tend to promote a kind of provincialism in attitude."

OBSERVATION 3. *Career programs and services can be categorized only in general terms.*

The multitude of tasks and functions performed by the variety of assistance units and practitioners can only be classified according to generic and vague descriptors.

**Career Counseling and Career Planning.** Self-assessment, diagnostic tests and aids, programs and resources on choice of major and career, occupational exploration, and career decision making are the core elements of this category. The focus of this category is college students' choices of and planning for careers that they will pursue during the working years of their lives.

**Job Search and Admissions Assistance.** Planning and execution of effective applications and search strategies are the essence of this category.

It includes services and resources such as credential files, on-campus interviewing, job vacancy notices, employment literature and videotapes, résumé referrals and data banks, and job fairs and conferences. The focus is on the transition of college students to postgraduate employment, education, or both.

**Constituent-Specific Career Programs.** Activities are designed to meet the career needs of specific student populations or to provide experience toward specific career paths. Special programs for special needs characterize this effort.

OBSERVATION 4. *Career programs and services, absent a traditional organizing theme or generally accepted professional practice, are usually organized according to local institutional needs and characteristics.*

The assignment of career functions on a college campus and the role that they play in the academic setting are, according to Shingleton and Fitzpatrick (1985), a function of the personality of the school, the career planning-placement needs, and the organizational structure of the university. Powell and Kirts (1980) have suggested that organizational structure is based on philosophy, cost, personnel available, faculty, and even the unique campus political environment.

The Carnegie Commission on Higher Education (1974) succinctly articulated a taxonomy of higher education institutions in 1970 to use in much of its analytical work. The work on this taxonomy and classification was undertaken because the mission and methods of institutions of higher education differ significantly. The previously cited observations confirm that the organization and role of career programs and services in these very different academic settings are very different!

OBSERVATION 5. *Career programs and services are so varied and diffuse that their organization represents a continuum of arrangements and assignments.*

The broader context of career assistance functions and Scott's (1983) findings indicate that virtually every college and university campus is, to some degree, decentralized. Organizational schemes and styles are thus a continuum with centralized and decentralized organizational forms, the generally accepted alternatives on the field (Shingleton and Fitzpatrick, 1985), as the ends of the spectrum. Contrast and comparison require examination of these two ends of the continuum to reveal how these categories combine into various modes of operation in between.

**Centralized, Concentrated End of the Career Assistance Spectrum.** Centralized styles are intended to be comprehensive, are usually assigned to student affairs, and are student services oriented. The college or university tends to amalgamate career assistance in an office that is centrally located and reports to a senior campus official. The American College Personnel Association's *Career Center Directors' National Data Bank* (Gast, 1991) indicates that 79 percent of the public institution respondents reported to the chief student affairs officer or an immediate subordinate. The inclusion of decentralized and academically specific career offices in CPC's (1991) *Career Planning and Placement Survey* revealed a lower percentage (62 percent) that reported through student affairs. Most often the orientation of practitioners in a centralized scheme is student developmental, thus its connection to student affairs and student services.

Liberal arts institutions are almost always centralized and provide career assistance through one office. This office has strong liaison and working relationships with the counseling office (and may be included in the counseling office), admissions, and faculty. Liberal arts colleges are usually centralized because there are only one or two people performing the role and they do everything. This organizational scheme is a function of size, cost, and personnel available.

Centralized, with connections to counseling and academic departments, is also the predominant style for comprehensive colleges and universities and doctorate-granting institutions. At larger institutions, counseling offices may assume a larger role in career planning, and special services offices may assume responsibility for minority student career development. Two-year institutions also tend toward a centralized organizational style in order to make career assistance convenient for adult and continuing learners within the time limitations faced by part-time and adult students.

Where decentralization exists within these primarily centralized institutions, it is almost always along functional lines rather than by academic affiliation. The case of Southern Illinois University at Carbondale (SIU-C) is illustrative. It is always dangerous to generalize from a specific example, but SIU-C seems to have something for everyone in its ongoing organization and reorganization of career planning and placement functions. According to Terence Buck (personal communication, June 18, 1992), head of student affairs, student services at SIU-C encompass placement, counseling, career development, testing, and the special needs of women, nontraditional students, and disabled students. Placement and counseling are the largest of the cadre. Career development was once attached to counseling and the testing services. Subsequently, career development was affiliated with placement when placement included the testing services. Career development is only one example of functional reassignment as SIU-C struggled to determine how the student services were most effectively aligned with each other. The result of the struggle was to give all of the services a separate identity and include them in a larger student services component of student affairs. The services are all located in one building, in one wing, adjacent to each other. This arrangement fosters greater interaction than was achieved with earlier combinations, yet it allows each unit to maintain some individuality and identity. A variety of functional combinations and locations were considered and implemented, consistent with factors of cost, efficiency, personnel, and effectiveness. The SIU-C experience illustrates that factors change over time and that the delivery of career services must be as dynamic as the institution's circumstances require.

**Decentralized, Dispersed End of the Career Assistance Spectrum.** Decentralized styles are specialized and usually organized by academic college or professional school (Greenberg, 1986). The distinguishing characteristic of this configuration is the professional linkage. Decentralized placement and career planning offices were developed from the close relationship between faculty of strong academic colleges and schools with an identifiable employer group. These faculty viewed the task of helping their students make the transition to corresponding employment arenas as their professional responsibility (Powell and Kirts, 1980). The decentralized office's connection with employers is exemplified by the relative importance and volume of on-campus recruiting compared to that of centralized schemes. In Greenberg's (1986) study of prerecruiting, nearly half of the decentralized respondents hosted more than one hundred employers annually, while only a third of the centralized respondents handled a similar volume.

Bechtel's (1991) survey of large midwestern research universities found that the presence of schools and colleges with strong ties to a profession or a specific employment arena seems to give rise to a specifically designated placement office for the professional school and a decentralized placement scheme at the institution. The survey highlighted the placement offices for agriculture, business, education, engineering, and law, where specifically designated offices existed for three-fourths of the respondents and for all the law schools.

Connections to a specific employment arena not only ease the transition of students but also foster strong continuing relationships between an identifiable employer group and the academic college or school. These connections have a related impact on fundraising, development, and research support through the potential partnerships of education with industry.

Preprofessional advising offices evolved in a manner similar to decentralized placement. The professional linkage predominates, with both connecting students with common academic majors to specific and related postgraduate endeavors. Premedical and prelaw advising services connect undergraduates to the professions of medicine and law, just as business and engineering career offices connect students to careers as accountants and engineers.

Research institutions with strong professional schools are usually large. Their enrollment numbers argue for a division into smaller units, thus decentralization. Research institutions have an average enrollment of 18,600 students, according to Carnegie Commission on Higher Education (1974) enrollment figures, and include academic schools and divisions with enrollments larger than most of the other Carnegie institutional types: liberal arts colleges, 954; two-year institutions, 2,213; and comprehensive universities and colleges, 5,522.

Bechtel's (1991, p. 2) survey of midwestern research institutions revealed that the number of placement offices at a large university is often only the "tip of the iceberg" regarding the actual number of offices and units that provide career assistance:

> The College Placement Council Membership Directory is not an inclusive list of each institution's career offices, and includes only the CPC members at an institution. Indeed, while the University of Illinois at Urbana-Champaign (UIUC) lists nine placement services in the Directory, there are actually 21. In addition to the 21 placement services, there are 12 more UIUC offices involved in career related programs. The CPC non-members, in addition to the smaller placement offices, include pre-professional advising offices, coop and internship offices, libraries, student unions and units that serve specific student constituencies. In similar fashion, the telephone survey revealed that 31 units are involved in providing career planning and placement services at Ohio State; Minnesota declares 16; Missouri, 22; Wisconsin, 23; Indiana, 17; Iowa, 21; Michigan, 10; Michigan State, 11; Northwestern, 11; Notre Dame, 12; Penn State, 16; and Purdue, 19.

Ohio State University (OSU) is an example of the proliferation of career assistance units on large, primarily decentralized campuses. OSU, with an enrollment of 54,000 (including 41,000 undergraduates), has sixteen academic colleges and eighteen academically specific career planning and placement offices. Primary responsibility for career counseling is held by the Counseling and Consultation Services Office, yet Arts and Sciences Career Services has a direct relationship with the university college (for undeclared students) and provides career counseling. University college advisers and those in the colleges of business, education, and human ecology also provide career counseling.

Career information collections exist in the OSU Counseling Office, the undergraduate library, and the Center for Teaching Excellence. Career assistance for minority students is the responsibility of the Office of Minority Student Services and of Counseling and Consultation Services. Special career assistance efforts are offered by other offices for Hispanic students, student athletes, and international students.

The College of Arts and Sciences at OSU (not its Career Services Office) has one prelaw adviser and two for the health professions. College honors offices give advice on graduate school admissions. Over thirty units are materially involved in providing some form of career assistance to OSU students (Bechtel, 1991).

**Combinations Between the Ends of the Career Assistance Organizational Spectrum.** Satellite, collegial, coordinated, and (sometimes) competitive arrangements exist on college and university campuses, usually large research institutions, that combine features of both ends of the continuum. Stemming from a centralized office for general administration, satellite offices may be located at branch campuses, at distant geographical locales, or within the institution in an academic department in order to provide convenient services and activities for students and improve the instrumentality of career assistance in relation to the institution's mission. Satellite offices are especially important for nontraditional students and commuter students whose time limitations are extreme.

The satellite style is actually a combined organizational scheme with a central base. The Pennsylvania State University system, in which the central office is located on the University Park campus and connected to satellite offices on each of the geographically distant two-year feeder campuses, is an example. The distinction between satellite and decentralized styles is based on the reporting line. A satellite reports directly to and is administratively affiliated with a centralized career planning and placement office; a decentralized office reports in an opposite direction up through the academic hierarchy to department heads and deans.

Coordinated and collegial systems are similar organizational arrangements. A coordinated system suggests that decentralized and centralized schemes exist simultaneously, meaning that certain functions, such as career counseling, may be centralized in one office, but other functions, such as placement and job search assistance, may be decentralized in a variety of academic and service units. Occasionally, one office coordinates the activities of others (Shingleton and Fitzpatrick, 1985). A coordinated system formally mandates the division of responsibility and assignment. A collegial system includes multiple career planning and placement offices that voluntarily cooperate in offering career services to students and employers (Powell and Kirts, 1980).

When combinations exist at liberal arts colleges, comprehensive universities, or doctorate-granting institutions, they usually result from the administration's directive to establish a division of labor and improve effectiveness and efficiency. The counseling office may do career planning, faculty committees or volunteers may provide preprofessional or pregraduate school advising, an internship unit coordinates with academic departments, and the career office does placement (Ginn, 1979). The division of labor is determined by functional orientations.

On larger research university campuses, committees and coordinating groups are sometimes formally appointed as the vehicles of coordination, but most coordination and cooperation occur informally (Scott, 1983). The University of Wisconsin at Madison has a long-standing, coordinating collegial group that includes placement officers, career counselors, academic advisers, adult education personnel, and others. Their ongoing activities include a coordinated event calendar, cosponsored career conferences, and mutually beneficial staff development programs.

Student clubs and organizations often complicate the cooperative spirit of a campus. Student groups, seeking an obvious path for themselves to the labor market or being dissatisfied because the career office is not doing enough for them, sponsor career programs and career fairs, inviting employers from their perceived corresponding employment arenas. Career planning and placement practitioners, scrambling to hold onto some semblance of centrality and instrumentality in their work, often cosponsor or administer activities with the student groups. Employers are hard-pressed not to attend a student group's activity and thus make multiple visits to the campus in an effort to also continue their regular relationship with the campus career planning and placement office. Michigan State University probably cosponsors more career conferences than does any other institution. They sponsor or cosponsor seventeen career fairs and conferences annually. Six are sponsored outright, and the rest are cosponsored with groups as diverse as Seniors in Business and the Department of Hotel, Restaurant, and Institutional Management (Bechtel, 1991).

Large or small enrollments, college or university designation, centralized or decentralized organization, "There is no substitution for each campus designing its own career development program around local needs and known effective responses" (Scott, 1983, p. 30).

OBSERVATION 6. *The importance of career programs and services varies according to the perspectives of the institutions' many constituencies.*

Each campus is unique, and, therefore, the institutional view of career assistance is localized and, in some cases, political (Powell and Kirts, 1980) or related to institutional needs rather than student needs (Scott, 1983).

**Importance of Career Assistance to Students and Families.** Johnson and Figler (1984, p. 464) capsulized the expectations of higher education with respect to careers: "Although it is seldom fully and overtly stated in a college catalogue, the belief is widespread that college courses are vocational, that they can be marketed in areas of employment . . . in the minds of many students, if not in the minds of the college as well."

Career services are important to parents, students, and tuition payers as a means of obtaining a return on their investment in education and as a route to a better life. Career services are important to returning students, nontraditional students, and part-time students, who are usually engaged in higher education as a transition to better-paying jobs and more fulfilling careers.

**Centrality of Career Assistance to the Institution.** Career planning and placement functions do not quite fit the centrality notion within the broad higher education purposes of teaching, research, and public service. Scott's (1983) report included a survey of presidents and chief academic and student affairs officers. Over 43 percent of the combined responses gave academic programs a higher priority than career planning and placement. Furthermore, some chief academic and student affairs officers reported that they would protect other programs under their purview before career planning and placement. Their view was in contrast to the presidents' broader and more inclusive perspective, which can be characterized as follows: "Although it is quite difficult to correlate college programs with job marketability, the belief dies hard. Colleges promote the vocational attitude, by elevating programs that are vocationally successful. In general, college has always been touted as the pathway to economic heaven" (Johnson and Figler, 1984, p. 464). Career services are not central, but they serve as means whereby teaching, research, and public service can be advanced and goals achieved.

**Public Accountability and the Balance of Priorities to Be Served.** A college remains a publicly accountable body, whether state supported or private, whose rules, procedures, and policies are set by legally constituted boards of trustees, governors, or regents (Benezel, 1981). Career concerns are central to the many publics that higher education serves: students, parents, legislators, businesses, and government. Higher education institutions exist to teach, conduct research, and respond to their publics' needs. Institutional governance, to carry out public policy, is often a balancing act of meeting the needs of the outer society that is served and the needs of college professionals, administrators, and faculty (Benezel, 1981). What seems central to outer society, career issues and the pathway to economic heaven for young people, is not always in accord with the teaching and research needs and wants of college professors.

The balance between outer society and institutional purposes and prerogatives may tip in favor of the concerns and perspectives of students, parents, and legislators in the accountability climate of the 1990s. State boards of higher education are now assuming a proactive role in institutional governance through accountability. Low-enrollment curricula are recommended for elimination, and others are directed to streamline or consolidate. Cost-effectiveness and productivity are the principal criteria, but another rationale is the potential "labor market" for these curricula and the demands reflected by student enrollment patterns.

Career services may be a means of connecting higher education and society at large, but many and most career service practitioners have not been vocal about how they help both students and their institution. The institutional perspective may have been that they are "nonprofessionals" who have nothing to contribute to resolution of the crises that colleges and universities face (Ginn, 1979). Yet the importance of career services and the work of career assistance practitioners, from an institutional perspective, is likely to grow.

## Conclusion

The same determining factors that gave rise to the continuum of organizational schemes for career programs and services at colleges and universities also reflect a diluted and ineffective response to the accountability challenges facing higher education: (1) a history of separateness and, sometimes, competition among career assistance providers; (2) multiple and diverse professional identities and affiliations of career assistance practitioners; and (3) local institutional characteristics, such as the size and character of the institution and the presence of professional schools, influencing both the organizational structure and importance of career programs and services. Scott's (1983, p. 31) observations, unfortunately, have proved prophetic: "Career planning and placement programs as well as the institutions that support them ostensibly exist to meet the needs of their immediate constituents as well as larger societal needs. Generally speaking, both have endeavored to meet those needs as they have seen them, however, they have been slow in identifying, acknowledging, and accommodating changing needs, especially rapidly emerging needs."

History is a prelude to the present—and the future. Given the history and circumstances of career assistance in higher education, the challenge of becoming a viable and important component in and instrumental to the future of higher education is enormous!

## References

Bechtel, D. S. *The Organization of Career Planning and Placement Functions at Selected Large, Midwestern Research Universities.* Champaign: Career Services Center, University of Illinois, 1991.

Benezel, L. T. "Governance." In A. W. Chickering and Associates, *The Modern American College: Responding to the New Realities of Diverse Students and a Changing Society.* San Francisco: Jossey-Bass, 1981.

Carnegie Commission on Higher Education. *A Classification of Institutions of Higher Education.* Princeton, N.J.: Carnegie Commission on Higher Education, 1974.

College Placement Council. *Career Counseling and Placement in Higher Education.* Bethlehem, Pa.: College Placement Council, 1970.

College Placement Council. *1991 Career Planning and Placement Survey.* Bethlehem, Pa.: College Placement Council, 1991.

Gast, L. K. *Career Center Directors' National Data Bank, Data Bank Survey (1988–90).* College Park, Md.: American College Personnel Association, 1991.

Ginn, A. J., Jr. "A Centralized Career Service: How Vital Is It?" *Journal of College Placement,* 1979, *40* (1), 23.

Gordin, E. E. "Counseling Point of View." In E. B. Williamson (ed.), *Trends in Student Personnel Work.* Minneapolis: University of Minnesota Press, 1949.

Greenberg, R. "The Current Status of, and Reactions to, the Issues of Prescreening, Preselection, and Prerecruiting." In *Special Report of the College Placement Council.* Bethlehem, Pa.: College Placement Council Foundation, 1986.

Hoppock, R. *Occupational Information.* New York: McGraw-Hill, 1963.

Johnson, C. A., and Figler, H. E. "Career Development and Placement Services in Postsecondary Institutions." In N. C. Gybers and Associates, *Designing Careers: Counseling to Enhance Education, Work, and Leisure.* San Francisco: Jossey-Bass, 1984.

Miles, J. H. "Serving the Career Guidance Needs of the Economically Disadvantaged." In N. C. Gybers and Associates, *Designing Careers: Counseling to Enhance Education, Work, and Leisure.* San Francisco: Jossey-Bass, 1984.

Mueller, K. H. *Student Personnel Work in Higher Education.* Boston: Houghton Mifflin, 1961.

Powell, C. R., and Kirts, D. K. *Career Services Today: A Dynamic College Profession.* Bethlehem, Pa.: College Placement Council, 1980.

Scott, G. J. *The Career Planning and Placement Office: Implications for the Future.* Bethlehem, Pa.: College Placement Council Foundation, 1983.

Shingleton, J. D., and Fitzpatrick, E. B. *Dynamics of Placement: How to Develop a Successful Career Planning and Placement Program.* Bethlehem, Pa.: College Placement Council Foundation, 1985.

Stephens, E. W. *Career Counseling and Placement in Higher Education: A Student Personnel Function.* Bethlehem, Pa.: College Placement Council, 1971.

DAVID S. BECHTEL *is director of the Career Services Center, including the Health Professions Information Office and the Office of Student Internships, at the University of Illinois, Urbana-Champaign, and serves as executive secretary of the university's Coordinating Committee on Career Planning and Placement, whose membership includes the career planning and placement personnel of the Urbana-Champaign campus.*

*This chapter describes the important elements of a comprehensive placement service and discusses a range of practical issues currently confronted by the placement profession.*

# Placement Services

*Richard A. Stewart*

The global recession of the late 1980s and early 1990s, followed by a very slow recovery, created significant economic problems for employers and institutions of higher education. A fundamental restructuring of business resulted in a decrease in the number of entry-level positions available to college graduates (particularly with the largest corporations) at a time when record numbers matriculated from the nation's colleges and universities. The result, of course, was anxiety and frustration among students, who assumed that a degree from a college or university was a guarantee of a job.

The same economic trends reduced the financial support to higher education, thus forcing institutions to do more with less. Among the changes forced on career planning and placement offices is the need for some institutions to charge fees to students, alumni, or employers for career and placement assistance that had been free in order to cover the shortfall in traditional funding patterns. The assessment of fees has also created negative reactions, particularly among students who believe that they have already paid enough.

This chapter pays particular attention to the task of defining placement issues in the 1990s. The issues covered include on-campus recruiting, employee-job matching systems, credential services, relationship of placement offices to development efforts, cooperative education and internship programs, alumni placement services, placement library material, and the involvement of third-party recruiters.

## Defining Placement

The word *placement* causes concern for many in the career planning and recruitment profession. For some, placement is referred to as the "P word," as if it were unspeakable. For others, it is the "bottom line" of the activities of their office and the only measure of success for their professional being.

For all, however, there has been a redefinition of the term. Historically, the term implied the activities of faculty and, later, placement officers in the proactive "selling" of individual graduates to prospective employers. Perhaps Professor Smith called a former student or professional colleague to alert him to a promising senior who should be given special consideration. And, from a historical perspective, the promising senior usually was a "him," since the phrase "old-boy network" derives from the tradition of males helping males. Similar marketing strategies were and to some extent are still employed today. The system and the word present an image of a passive student and an active college or university official who "places" the student in the "right" position.

In the dynamic employment market of the 1990s, with over one million degree recipients entering the work force each year, it is impossible for university and college officials to "place" every student. Beyond the logistical problems, there are more important issues of personal responsibility and the development of life skills by the students. With the rapid pace of career changes and the anticipation that today's graduate will perhaps have three or more careers and seven to fifteen jobs during the course of his or her working life, who will place the student three or fifteen or even twenty-five years into the future? Certainly, it cannot be, nor should it be, the placement office from the alma mater.

What, then, does placement mean in the context of the marketplace today and into the twenty-first century? It means preparing students to repeatedly place themselves throughout their working lives (Powell and Kirts, 1980). For the growing number of returning students, or those sometimes referred to as adult learners, mature students, or nontraditional students, the placement may not be the first time for each, but in the 1990s and beyond there is no guarantee that it will be the only time. The placement service functions best if it provides students with a realistic view of the world of work, the ability to assess their own strengths, weaknesses, desires, and goals, and then helps them as they develop plans for self-placement. This function requires an awareness of and sensitivity to the needs of the nontraditional student. Career counselors experience varying degrees of concern expressed by this student cohort regarding their ability to successfully compete with traditional college graduates. Likewise, the placement office staff must be prepared to deal with interviewers who may, for the first time, find a candidate for an entry-level position who is in his or her thirties, forties, or beyond. And with the implementation of the Americans with Disabilities Act of 1992, placement offices and employers have begun to deal with the needs of a growing number of students previously not included in the traditional student category. As some schools and employers have found, "reasonable accommodation" need not be costly or time-consuming, but it must be accomplished.

Contrary to the expectations of many students and, perhaps, the hopes of families, employment in the first career job is not guaranteed by graduation day. Estimates vary greatly for employment at graduation. At Purdue University, for example, a survey of postgraduation plans is conducted just prior to every graduation. With the cooperation of the registrar's office as well as other departments involved in the commencement ceremonies, a 90 percent response rate to each survey is typically achieved. From these surveys, it is obvious that the acceptance of employment prior to graduation varies depending on the supply and demand for each academic area. Nursing students in the late 1980s and early 1990s reported an employment rate of over 80 percent prior to graduation, while some majors in nontechnical areas reported a rate of less than 30 percent. It should be noted that placement for some academic areas may primarily be in jobs, while in others graduate or professional school is the placement of choice.

The Commission on Professionals in Science and Technology (1992) has reported on the positive job outlook for nursing students as well as the loss of many entry-level positions for college graduates resulting from the continuing recession. Since there is no national data base to provide actual figures, we can only surmise that some high estimates of placement reflect the institutions' concern for recruiting new students and thus are not reliable employment figures.

There have been a number of attempts by the federal government to mandate the maintenance of placement statistics. Some attempts may have been the results of charges of false advertising by proprietary schools, and, of course, some concerns were based on the high default rate for student loans when graduates are unemployed (Breneman, 1991). Even though much of the focus has been on proprietary schools, all postsecondary education institutions will be covered under proposed regulations.

In addition to government interest in placement, some organizations have attempted to "measure" placement (along with financial aid counseling, student health centers, and so on). For example, the National Association of College and University Business Officers (NACUBO) is conducting the Benchmarking Project. This pilot program attempts to quantify and measure success by collecting data on variables such as budgets and students' ratios of interviews to placement dollars allocated. "The objective is to provide comparative data that will stimulate the search for best practices in administrative operations. . . . Benchmarking will play a major role in helping the higher education industry respond to increasing pressures for enhanced quality and lower costs" (NACUBO, 1992, p. 1).

Is it any wonder that the "P word" raises concern in the minds of many practitioners? While many employers refer to the campus offices with which they work as placement offices, few staff members in these campus facilities see themselves in what is construed as an outmoded, if not discredited, role. In the College Placement Council (1991) survey, 93 percent of the respondents indicated that placement of graduates into full-time employment was a service offered by their respective office, whereas only 10 percent of the respondents used the word placement in the title of the office. An additional 30 percent used placement in conjunction with other words such as career planning or counseling, leaving 60 percent who used other terminology that generally excluded the word placement.

## On-Campus Recruiting

Regardless of the organizational structure within career services, that is, whether centralized or decentralized, comprehensive or single purpose, many, if not the majority, of these offices deal with the issue of on-campus recruiting. Obviously, the schools whose mission includes a strong vocational component, for example, M.B.A. programs, engineering, and sciences, are more concerned with on-campus recruiting than are those colleges and universities whose mission can more accurately be defined as preprofessional. Among the latter group, many liberal arts colleges see their role as preparation for graduate or professional studies and, therefore, are not as concerned with initial job placement resulting from on-campus recruitment activities.

Historically, on-campus recruiting has served the entry-level hiring needs of two major employer groups. First, there are the local employers who want to tap the readily available pool of talent in their own community. Small firms have competed successfully on campus for talent, particularly among those students who wish to remain in the same geographical region that served their education needs. Second, there are the national firms who seek to fill thousands of entry-level openings. For many large institutions, on-campus recruiting was formerly synonymous with the hosting of Fortune 500 corporations that had a seemingly insatiable need for new talent. A pattern developed over a period of forty or fifty years that resulted in complacency and faith that the future would be the same as the past. It appears, however, that the 1990s and beyond will see a shift in employer emphasis from a "shotgun" approach, where large employers go to many universities and colleges to hire, to a "rifle" approach, where even the largest firms scale down the number of campus visits to a few targeted schools. For example, some large firms that formerly interviewed on as many as two hundred campuses from coast to coast have cut their targeted schools to under seventy-five and hope to reduce further the number to twenty or thirty major "suppliers."

The ease and convenience of access to employers is one of many benefits for students enrolled in an institution with a well-developed on-campus recruiting program. For the rest of the campus community, obvious spin-offs from a successful placement program include the opportunity for interaction

between corporate America and academe, which frequently enh&
rate financial support of the college or university. Even though
implicit or explicit quid pro quo for the interaction with the caree
office, the reality is that if employers hire from a particular schoo\
more likely to provide financial support to that school.

The goal of having the right student in the right room with the right
employer at the right time seems straightforward and perhaps simple to
accomplish. However, experience has shown that the process can have
unlimited variations and is influenced by many factors, such as the economy
as well as the goals of the particular school or the placement office. Obviously,
employers want the best candidates available from whatever sources they
deem appropriate to fill the needs of their organization. Never does a
placement office find an employer seeking the worst students, with the
lowest grade point averages. Employers do not seek students who are
unmotivated and inarticulate and who do not know what they want to do.
Even in difficult economic times, employer demand for the top students
remains strong.

To respond to the needs of the employer "customer," universities and
colleges have developed a variety of systems and procedures. There is no
one system that is preferable or superior to others. The size of the student
population, the staffing of the placement service, and the facilities and
funds available determine which system works best in a given situation.
Over the years, several different procedures have evolved for handling on-
campus recruiting. A review of the most common of these procedures is
presented here.

For thirty or forty years, beginning in the 1930s, the most prevalent
method for scheduling interviews between students and employers was to
post job information so that students who were interested in a given position,
had the requested major, and believed that they were qualified could
schedule interviews on a first-come, first-served basis. This process worked
relatively well for many institutions for many years; however, the rapid
growth of higher education created a major problem in the decades of the
1960s and 1970s. Frequently, the number of students interested in and
qualified for interviews with a given employer exceeded the interviewing
time made available by the employer. Placement services were faced with
overwhelming numbers of students who lined up, sometimes twenty-four
hours in advance, when employer interview schedules were posted. Students
complained of having to spend hours in line without any assurance of an
opportunity to interview. Students were also unable to participate in extracurricular activities, study, or work during the time that they were in line in
order to obtain a chance for an interview.

A variety of solutions to this problem evolved and continue to be refined.
Some offices have retained the first-come, first-served format, believing that
this system at least treats all students the same. In some schools, lotteries or

drawings are used to allocate relatively scarce interview time. The obvious drawback of this procedure is the very nature of a random system, that is, some students are just left out. Other offices have instituted computerized sign-up systems to help allocate interviews on a bidding basis. In this type of system, students are each given a number of "points" (say, five hundred) to be used to "purchase" interview time with employers of interest. Students thus control how much they are willing to bid to obtain interviews with particular employers. A student can almost guarantee at least one interview by using all of the points for one employer. However, most students estimate the interest in (competition for) several employers and try to optimize the use of their points. In some complex variations of this system, students are informed of the minimum number of points currently needed to obtain a given interview. Obviously, the use of computers as well as electronic communication with students is essential for the successful implementation of such a bidding system. And some schools use forced-ranking algorithms that schedule interviews based on student interest, while ensuring an equitable distribution of available interview times to as many students as possible throughout the year.

For many employers, the overwhelming number of candidates seeking to interview with their organization resulted in assessment of the cost-benefit factors involved in various recruiting systems. For some employers, review of candidate credentials and preselection of those whom they wished to interview made more sense than use of first come, first served; random assignment; bidding; or computer algorithms. Campus career services offices responded in a variety of ways to the employers' need to manage more effectively the number of interviews. Some schools said no to any form of employer preselection. Other schools were willing to accommodate at least 50 percent employer preselection and 50 percent student-driven selection. And still other schools went to 100 percent employer preselection as a way of assuring each candidate that he or she had an equal chance to be selected. There have been no comprehensive studies comparing the long-term effectiveness of the various systems; however, many employers maintain that in slow-growth times, preselection is the most cost-effective method of ensuring that the right student has the opportunity to interview with the right employers.

Some career planning officers have expressed concern that the practice of allowing total employer preselection encourages passive behavior from students, who may learn late in the school year that they are not going to be selected and that they have missed opportunities to act on their own behalf. In effect, reliance on employer preselection has many of the same drawbacks as the old placement syndrome, in which faculty and other university officials controlled the employment fate of graduates.

Regardless of the method used for developing an interview schedule on campus, it is important to realize that the environment in which the interview takes place influences employers' perceptions of the college or university as a whole and not just the office in which they are interviewing. While every placement service would like to have exceptionally fine facilities, adequate interview rooms, and plenty of space for career resources used by students, most schools in fact make do with inadequate space. Generally speaking, placement offices have not ranked high on the list of institutional priorities for space allocation. Many schools must make do with facilities that are decades old. Very few placement services have had the luxury of designing their own facilities with no restrictions on square footage or dollar investment to accomplish the task. Employers who visit more than one or two campuses can quickly assess and compare the importance placed on the employment of graduates at a given college or university simply by observing the physical facilities of the placement service. At some institutions, there may be thirty or forty private interview rooms designed specifically for the purpose of student-employer interaction. In some cases, each room is equipped with a computer and a telephone. In addition, the overall facilities are spacious, well lit, and well staffed. In contrast, there are schools where, at best, interviews take place in faculty offices, borrowed classrooms, or any other spaces that can be expropriated for the interview day.

## Employee-Job Matching Systems

Concurrent with the increase in the numbers of graduates, and the more highly targeted employer recruiting efforts, came the recognition of an opportunity for the development of employee-job matching systems. Entrepreneurs envisioned a lucrative market if they could develop easy-to-use, relatively inexpensive matching systems for employers faced with the task of matching job openings with thousands of applicants.

One of the first attempts in this area was in the 1960s when the College Placement Council utilized a computer matching system. The system, Graduate Résumé Accumulation and Distribution, was designed to assist employers by matching job requirements to alumni qualifications. In the years that followed, seemingly hundreds of other attempts to provide *the* matching system were brought to the marketplace, all eventually fading from view. How many long-time recruitment and career planning professionals recall Compujob, or Chet Huntley's (of television news fame) attempt to solve the matching problems for students, schools, alumni, and employers? Currently, there are no doubt others who are working on yet more systems. By the end of the 1980s, some employers had successfully developed in-house tracking and matching systems. With the advent of computerized sign-up systems in some placement offices, more schools began to look to the computer as a way to manage large amounts of data about their clients. This step naturally led to the development of electronic matching systems based in the placement offices.

In 1985, a consortium of employers and schools in the Midwest College Placement Association developed a computerized student résumé system, which included matching capabilities to assist placement offices in identifying students whose backgrounds and interests most nearly met the job specifications provided by employers. The system was adapted by the College Placement Council and marketed under the name VitaQuik. As with many commercial ventures, VitaQuik did not meet the test of the marketplace, but it did add to the growing interest in computerization as a tool for facilitating employee-job matching systems.

More important, VitaQuik spawned the first interest in computer standards for the electronic interchange of student data from placement offices to employers. A group of employers and placement offices recognized the importance of a standard if there was to be compatibility between schools and employers using different hardware and software configurations for matching systems, information transfer, and application tracking systems. The Data Sheet Interchange Standard, or DASIS, was developed in 1988. The use of a standard will prevent the computer equivalent of a Tower of Babel as computers become as commonplace as telephones and fax machines in career planning, placement, and recruitment. With the capability of personal computers increasing while costs are decreasing, electronics will be in and paper will be out as the profession moves into the twenty-first century.

Many schools utilize electronic résumé books to deliver student résumés to employers. The electronic systems are more flexible and less expensive for both placement offices and employers. In addition, several national data bases allow employer access to student résumé data for job matching purposes. Among the current systems are kiNexus, a floppy-disk-based matching system; the College Recruitment Database, an online, real-time matching system available to employers who subscribe to the Human Resources Information Network; and Peterson's Connexion (see Resources at the end of this chapter).

As in the previous two decades, new systems are introduced regularly, but the marketplace determines the viability of the systems. The only sure thing is continued progress in the use of computer technology in the arena of employee-job matching. The next level of activity apparently will focus on online rather than floppy disk systems.

## Credential Services

For years, one function associated with placement offices has been the provision of credentials to prospective employers. The value of maintaining letters of recommendation provided by faculty, employers, and family acquaintances has been viewed with some degree of skepticism by many recipients of these glowing reports on the outstanding candidates recommended. Perhaps no single event did more to dampen the enthusiasm for the maintenance of credentials than the Family Educational Rights and Privacy Act, also known as the Buckley amendment. In effect, this federal legislation put a chill on the attempts at objectivity by those asked to write letters of recommendation. While students can and do waive their right to see recommendations, only the foolhardy would put negative comments in writing with little regard for the legal ramifications should the contents of the recommendation be made known to the applicant. A number of placement offices serving primarily business, industry, and government have drastically reduced, or in many cases eliminated, the maintenance of recommendations. As far back as the 1960s, a Midwest College Placement Association survey (Paquette, 1966) of employer use of references indicated that fewer than 30 percent of the employers considered letters of reference a major factor in the selection process. Employers preferred to focus on the academic achievements of candidates, their abilities in the interviews, and their work experience.

The last bastion of a deep commitment to full credentials appears to be in the employment of elementary and secondary school teachers and administrators. Perhaps the fact that many school corporations are not funded sufficiently to provide the opportunity for significant on-campus recruiting, or hosting of candidates for on-site interviews, explains the continuing reliance on documentation. Or perhaps it is the attitude of "just the way we've always done it" that has driven many placement offices to maintain and manipulate thousands of pieces of paper for decades.

While computerization has helped to streamline the credentials process for recent graduates, many schools wrestle with what to do with the file cabinets full of recommendations from graduates who still might want to reactivate their files and again use the glowing comments provided years or decades ago. Anecdotally, I personally became suspicious of the value of extensive credential files during the first days of space flight. One of the illustrious alumni of the university at which I worked had gained national prominence for a trip into outer space, and the media descended on campus to interview any or all who had had contact with this individual as a student. One professor related to the media how he always knew that this graduate would go far (no pun intended) and do well. The next day I checked that individual's recommendations in the credential file for the astronaut and found the following remarks: "Average student, average grades, will probably make the military his career." So much for foresight and hindsight. Shortly thereafter our office decided that comments made by faculty years earlier frequently had little relationship to the current-day performance of our graduates. Ten file cabinets full of recommendations were eliminated, as was a lot of paper shuffling. Our students continue to find employment and are successful in spite of the lack of a credential file system.

It is incumbent on the placement office, however, to ensure that sufficient data are available on candidates to assist in employer assessment. Easy access to academic transcripts and comprehensive résumés including accomplishments in academics, extracurricular activities, and work settings is a must. As has been mentioned, many schools have gone to student data bases or computerized résumés to facilitate the communication of information about students to employers seeking candidates. However, as several employers agreed during a meeting regarding what should be included in a student résumé, "more is not necessarily better." It is the quality and accessibility of information on the candidate that count, not the volume.

## Relationship of Placement Offices to Development Efforts

Every college and university has come to the realization that funding through traditional sources, for example, tuition, taxes, federal grants, and alumni giving, is not sufficient to meet the increasing costs of higher education. When funds to maintain quality programs are not forthcoming from students, alumni, and state legislatures, it is not surprising that the thoughts of administrators turn to corporate America. After all, a vast majority of graduates go to work in the business community, so why not ask for support for the educational preparation of those graduates who are the future of the corporations? A well-educated employee can be a more productive employee; therefore, corporations should have a vested interest in the quality of the future work force. Many employers recognize the need to support major suppliers to the corporate head count, some of which are the alma maters of high-ranking executives.

In recent years, campus development offices have discovered that data regarding target employers can be enhanced by working with the placement offices. In many institutions, hardly a week goes by without at least one call to the placement office asking for the recruiting record of company X, Y, or Z. The information requested includes the number of hires in the prior year, the total number of graduates in the company, and the company's recent interviewing activity. Placement office staff generally can provide some if not all of the desired information and certainly understand that the development effort, if successful, can benefit the total institution.

The rub comes when overzealous individuals involved in development imply a quid pro quo arrangement involving the placement of students. It is not unknown for development representatives to appear in corporate offices with résumés of high-profile, high-energy, high-achieving students, noting that these are just a sample of what the school produces: "You can help us do a better job (and, by the way, have access to these kinds of students) by supporting our development efforts." As brazen as this approach may sound, it happens—and it works! The unfortunate side of this scenario is the manipulation of students for purposes other than their career development. Students have reported that professors or administrators have strongly encouraged them to interview with certain organizations and implied that if they want to get along, they have to go along. Students react to this sort of pressure with appreciation if they are having difficulty finding employment, frustration if their interviews do not prove productive, or anger if they have absolutely no interest in the organizations or the career opportunities presented. The old-boy network is alive and well on campus, even if the placement office is not involved in the situation.

Many academic units have developed "associates programs" to provide special service to donors. Usually listed among the benefits of belonging to a program is "access to top students." While there is certainly nothing illegal, immoral, or unethical in assisting employers, this activity is a problem when the impression is created that employers must belong to an associates program in order to have access to students. No doubt many placement directors at technical universities can recall more than one telephone call or conversation with an employer who asked, rather plaintively, "If I don't join, does that mean I can't hire good students from your institution?" Fortunately, the more blatant abuses of the placement-development relationship are rare. The best avoidance technique for placement offices is the establishment of a good rapport with the development staff. With a discussion of the danger of offending many employers to benefit a few, misunderstandings can be avoided. As in many other endeavors, it is best to ensure that all parties understand that short-term gains can sometimes create long-term problems.

## Cooperative Education and Internship Programs

Some placement services are responsible for cooperative education programs and internships. A few definitions may help clarify the variety of programs. Cooperative education can range from an alternating work-study arrangement for one, two, or three semesters or quarters, to programs that require a five-year commitment from the student to obtain a bachelor's degree and a certificate for cooperative education. Some schools require students to participate in cooperative education, while at others it is strictly a voluntary situation. In addition to the work experience gained by the student for his or her participation, the financial rewards make cooperative education an attractive option for today's student.

In some schools, cooperative education activities are separate from the placement office. This situation is unfortunate, since there is a natural link for employers between seeking students for the cooperative experience and seeking full-time employees from the senior-year cohort. If the placement service is not directly responsible for the cooperative program, every effort should be made to maintain open lines of communication between the two offices, since they are working toward the same goal: a productive career for the graduate.

Internships range from nonpaid activities for the experience only, through programs for academic credit, to the more familiar summer jobs in career-related positions. The role of the placement office can vary from reactive, where openings are posted for students to use their own initiative, to proactive, which entails job development to convince employers to hire students. Like any other job development program, internship development can be a time-consuming and expensive activity. In the 1990s, an increasing number of placement offices will look at marketing strategies and job development activities to increase the opportunities for their students and alumni. A well-run internship-development program can become part of an overall job development effort. The limiting factor is staff time; however, the creative use of students and alumni can accomplish a great deal. For example, Rensselaer Polytechnic Institute's "job-a-thon," which uses students to call alumni to obtain pledges of job assistance for the institute's students in internships and full-time employment, will no doubt be tried on other campuses.

## Alumni Placement Services

While not directly related to current student needs, many placement services have found alumni placement activities to be productive. This is particularly evident for the recent graduate who has been unsuccessful in finding employment prior to graduation and is in need of assistance in shifting from the world of academics to the world of work. Assistance for alumni ranges from counseling to job-listing notification systems, résumé referrals, and interview schedules. In a declining economy, the distinction between services provided to students and the services needed by new alumni becomes blurred.

Alumni placement activities can also extend to midlife career changers and those who, voluntarily or not, face early retirement. Some alumni placement services, of course, are an adjunct of the alumni association; however, on many campuses, it is the responsibility of the student placement office to provide services to alumni. While there is a clear need to expand efforts to assist alumni, many placement offices are facing decreases in funding. Unfortunately, as a result, the offices are forced to charge fees for alumni services, which can create negative feelings among those who are already frustrated by unemployment.

Alumni placement assistance can generally be divided into four categories: counseling, résumé referral, job-opening notification, and interviewing. The geographical location of a school plays an important part in the expectations of alumni regarding services that should be provided. Obviously, a school located in a major metropolitan area with a high number of alumni nearby experiences a greater demand for services from alumni than does a rural school isolated from a major concentration of alumni.

Another factor in the expectations of alumni regarding placement assistance is the relationship that the individuals had with the office when they were students. Younger alumni, in particular, may contact their alma maters if, during their student years, they believed that they obtained help in securing that all-important first job.

If a strong counseling relationship was developed between students and the placement staff, it is logical that graduates will seek assistance from a familiar source, particularly if they live near the school and especially if graduation was not too far in the past. With high unemployment among recent graduates seemingly on the increase during the beginning of the 1990s, large numbers of requests for counseling can create problems, but they may also provide opportunities. Arizona State University, a school with a high number of alumni in the area, has instituted a fee schedule for alumni services. The fees have the potential to generate sufficient income to allow the placement office to provide counseling and other alumni services not possible with a budget supported solely by state funds. The initiative for this fee structure came from the state legislature, which directed all three state schools to focus efforts on current students and to charge alumni for services.

While a résumé referral service for alumni would appear to be an excellent way to develop employer support and at the same time provide a needed service, the issues of funding and staffing again frequently weigh against the successful implementation of a productive service. Can the school charge alumni a fee for referring their résumé and not end up becoming just another employment agency? Clearly, if the graduates of a given school are in high demand and low supply, employers can and will pay to receive résumés. The matching of alumni résumés to employer specifications is an expensive and time-consuming job if it is done correctly.

For a number of years, Purdue University sold a publication of mini-résumés to employers so that they could do the screening. Full résumés for specific alumni would be provided when the employer requested them by code numbers. Employers liked this system, but editing of the résumés proved too labor-intensive. It also served alumni in high-demand areas very well and did very little for those whose majors were in oversupply.

One bright spot in the area of résumé referral for alumni is the computer. With computer-based résumés, much of the labor-intensive work of matching jobs and people can be reduced. This may lead to more emphasis on alumni résumé referral but will do little to change the inherent supply-demand issues. As mentioned earlier, a number of the commercial systems designed to aid students are also targeting the alumni résumé referral market.

If alumni résumé referral is not a viable option for a placement office, a job-opening notification system may be an acceptable alternative. While the editing of a job bulletin requires staff time, it usually is less labor-intensive than the editing of résumés or the matching of résumés to job specifications. Also, by providing alumni with current openings, the placement service can provide graduates with a look at actual conditions in the job market. At Purdue, some alumni complain to our office upon receipt of our twice-monthly job bulletin that there are too many positions for some majors and not enough for their own. This provides an entrée for counseling regarding supply and demand, and the opportunity to discuss skills-based rather than major-based job searches.

It has been the experience of a number of placement offices, including Purdue's, that alumni are willing to subscribe to a job bulletin if they believe that the price is right. Purdue has found that offering a three-month, six-issue subscription for one price and a six-month, twelve-issue subscription at a discount is acceptable to alumni.

Another method to consider is voice mail through touch-tone telephone listings. San Francisco State University has instituted a program whereby, for a small fee, incoming calls regarding positions can be listed in the caller's own voice. The system was developed primarily to handle the large volume of local positions and to disseminate information to a nonresident student population, but the concept can be utilized as a stand-alone voice-mail system for alumni only. The University of Virginia, among others, has a similar system for alumni.

A variety of payment schemes can be designed to incorporate voice-mail job notification, including billing through "900" numbers, granting of telephone personal identification numbers for a fee, or charging employers for the listing through a billing system. Regardless of the payment method, voice mail reduces staff time and has the added benefit of accessibility to alumni twenty-four hours a day, seven days a week.

With any job notification system, placement offices must develop policies regarding the listing of employment agency openings. At Purdue, for instance, we found that free listings from agencies grew to the point that we questioned whose needs were being met. In 1991, agencies were informed that since our goal is to serve our alumni and those employers who hire Purdue graduates, we were discontinuing the free agency listings and instituting a $50 "advertising" fee. Agency listings dropped from seventy-three per issue to one. For those agencies who pay to list, our fee is a bargain (and it does generate money for alumni placement activities), since one successful placement can generate many times the investment in the advertisement for the agency.

Perhaps the most difficult service to provide—or, rather, to deny—is on-campus interviewing for newly graduated alumni. Schools with very active on-campus interviewing programs frequently deal with unemployed graduates who, after spending four or more years and thousands of dollars, are surprised (or angry or frustrated) if they can no longer schedule interviews through the placement service. It does not help to point out to them that they no longer receive the student rate for services from other departments, such as the health service and the athletic department.

The solution to this problem must be comfortable to each school based on its situation. For some, such as Georgia Institute of Technology, alumni may continue to schedule interviews on campus for up to three months after graduation; while for others, such as Purdue, alumni cannot schedule on-campus interviews unless an academic department requests a waiver based on unique circumstances. With declining on-campus interviewing activity, it is difficult to provide sufficient on-campus interviewing opportunities to current candidates let alone to untold numbers of alumni.

While there no doubt are a number of alumni placement offices off campus, the University of Illinois Alumni Career Center in Chicago is a model worthy of investigation by any school seriously interested in assisting alumni who are concentrated in a major metropolitan area removed from the main campus. Services of this office range from on-site interviewing, through maintenance of résumé books, to a job fair for experienced alumni. The services are provided to all graduates of the University of Illinois in Urbana-Champaign and in Chicago.

## Placement Library Material

Today's placement library generally contains information on employers as well as many other career resources. Traditionally, employer information has been thought of in terms of recruitment brochures or annual reports. Today, career libraries have been expanded to include employer videotapes and personal computer disks complete with graphics programs. In a large central placement office, one may find two thousand or more corporate and government agency recruitment folders. Included are annual reports and product information, as well as community and chamber of commerce materials. In addition, it is not uncommon to find between four hundred and six hundred videotapes and numerous audiotapes.

Beyond the thousands of items to be maintained on behalf of employers, the placement service library is responsible for career resource materials, including books on job seeking techniques, résumé writing, and job strategies. The placement library also subscribes to various directories, journals, and other publications that can assist students in a job search. There are untold numbers of directories published by professional societies and commercial publications listing employers by city, region, and state.

Over the past five to seven years, there has been a proliferation of magazines targeted specifically to job seeking college students. Some of the magazines have relatively stable histories, whereas others come and go. While some publications are general in nature and focus on a variety of career opportunities, the great majority of publications target women, minorities, engineers, M.B.A.'s, retail majors, the disabled, and other specific audiences. Most of the publications have one thing in common—more advertising than useful career information and little that cannot be found in traditional career planning and placement office handouts. Nonetheless, there are some pearls of wisdom in these publications, and they can be of assistance to the placement staff and the student population in general.

No doubt the organizations advertising in the various publications envision distribution systems on campus that ensure the delivery of their message to the appropriate students. And, of course, advertisers expect that the publications will appear on schedule. Unfortunately, for overworked and understaffed placement offices, the delivery system of choice is usually that of putting such material on public display racks or, worse, leaving it in boxes for students or parents or visitors to pick up as the spirit moves them. If the school is fortunate enough to have a mailbox for each student and the placement office has sufficient staff, distribution can be more targeted. With the advent of computerized registration procedures, it is also possible to provide mailing labels to publishers; however, many placement officials are reluctant to hand over mailing lists or labels since they fear misuse of the information.

For large central placement offices in particular, there is no way in which the placement staff can ensure that the publications are distributed to the correct students. Moreover, based on the date of receipt of some of the publications, they might as well be consigned directly to the recycling effort to at least achieve some benefit to society, if not the publisher or advertisers. In the marketplace of the 1990s, notwithstanding the sad state of the economy, it is naive to believe that very many high-demand, high-technology-minded, high-performance students are eagerly pursuing advertisements one or two months prior to graduation. Perhaps there would be some benefit if the publications arrived early in the fall semester rather than late in the spring.

Most placement offices have faced the problem of receiving a growing number of media pieces at a time when space is at a premium, staff is even more hard to come by, and budgets are shrinking. For most placement offices, the dilemma is how to maintain all of the information that can be of assistance to the staff and the students and still find room for staff, student workers, computers, interviewers, and the student clients.

North Carolina State University has established a policy that only publications preapproved by the placement center will be accepted by the university mail service and all others will be returned to the senders. At Purdue, this would mean that only four or five of the fifteen or so publications arriving at the loading docks of the university would make it to our office. This may be a good idea, certainly with respect to some of the publications that we have received a week or so before the spring semester ends.

Depending on the location of the placement service, it may be possible to partner the placement library with the institution's library. There are obvious advantages both to the library and to the placement office in this arrangement. Since placement offices generally are short on space and staff to maintain the materials, there is an advantage to having the library professionals handle this task for them. The second and perhaps the most important benefit centers on the accessibility of the materials at times when students may want to use them. Most placement offices are open forty to forty-five hours a week, generally during a five- or six-day period. Libraries, on the other hand, are open seven days a week, from twelve to twenty-four hours per day. If the placement library materials are maintained in a partnership arrangement with the general library, the students and the placement office are winners.

The library can be a winner in this partnership by incorporating career and employer information into their normal operations, thus increasing student use of and familiarity with the library system. If the hundreds of corporate and agency binders are maintained as reserved books, they may be checked out in the same manner as any other reserved book. A side benefit of using the library is the reduction of pilferage and theft that is common to most placement libraries, along with a built-in system to measure the use of the materials.

With the increase in the use of video materials, it has become difficult and expensive for a placement office alone to have available a sufficient number of video players in one location. Again, a well-designed library may contain twenty or thirty video machines and can check out the placement videos during a twelve- to twenty-four-hour period, seven days per week. Even though 1991–1992 was a bad recruiting year, the Purdue Library, on behalf of the university placement service, checked out reserved employer literature over twenty thousand times in ten months and checked out employer videos more than six thousand times. There is absolutely no way in which this could be done with our limited placement staff, limited space, and shrinking budget. As employers move to more creative marketing strategies utilizing personal computer disks with color graphics and animation, the libraries with computer availability can maintain the disks in the same manner as books and videotapes.

## Involvement of Third-Party Recruiters

Among the many changes affecting the traditional placement office is increased interaction with third-party recruiters. Third-party recruiters are individuals or organizations such as employment agencies, search firms, and résumé referral firms, who recruit candidates for employment opportunities on behalf of others. In the past, many placement offices refused to even consider working with third-party professionals, insisting that only the ultimate hiring entities would be provided service. While this is still the preference of many placement officials, the reality of the job market in poor economic times is that a job is a job is a job. The source of the job is not as important as the fact of its existence. In dealing with a third-party professional, the task of the placement office is to accommodate the third party without compromising professional ethics. This can be accomplished by ensuring, through written documentation, that the third party is in fact the agent of a particular employer and that the individuals involved have the authority to work exclusively for that employer. If this documentation can be provided, there should be no other reason to limit a student's access to employers simply because the employers chose to contract their college recruiting to specialty firms.

It may come to pass that numerous employers will consider contracting for college recruiting, much as they now contract for engineering or computer skills. The "just-in-time" philosophy in the manufacturing sector can be applied in recruitment with the use of agency personnel rather than full-time staff. Such an arrangement helps corporations manage head counts and eliminates the need to downsize the recruiting staff when there is little or no need for new college talent. A pilot of this concept was announced in 1992 when IBM created a subsidiary company, Employment Solutions, and transferred much of its recruiting effort out of the parent company.

As the world changes, placement must change. In reality, many third-party professionals are more concerned with the experienced job seeker than with the new graduate. After all, agency fees are based on employee salary, and it is certainly more lucrative to collect a fee for a $75,000-a-year executive than a $15,000-a-year new graduate. Again, the placement office must set ground rules for the interaction. Some offices may be more comfortable listing third-party opportunities with a disclaimer to students and alumni who may review the listings that the placement office does not endorse the agency. The placement office does have an obligation to educate students and alumni about the potential problems of signing contracts with third-party agencies without understanding the terms of the contracts. Beyond that, each placement office has to decide whether to be proactive in sorting out the candidates desired by the third party, or just reactive in posting information and allowing alumni or students to make the final judgment as to their interest in the agency.

## Conclusion

The placement services of today are certainly different from those of the past forty years. We have come from a time of small numbers of graduates (mostly white and male) and the general perception of an active placement effort on behalf of students, to a situation where the large number of graduates and the ever-changing job market demand that we prepare students to be more proactive in placing themselves the first time and probably many more times. As the number of graduates has grown and resources for placement offices have diminished or at best remained stagnant, the placement office has had to face the challenge of adopting ever-changing strategies to reach an increasingly diverse student population that is confronting a less expansionary and hence more competitive job market. While there will probably be shortages of graduates in certain academic areas in the future, it appears that in general there will continue to be an oversupply in many fields for years to come.

Through increased use of technology, including computers, fax machines, and video and voice mail systems, the placement office can overcome the multiple problems of limited resources, large student-to-staff ratios, and uncertain employer demand. This task, however, will require continual reassessment of funding sources. Gone, perhaps forever, are the days when institutional funding was sufficient to accomplish the mission of the placement office. In the fiscal environment of the 1990s, fees from students, employers, alumni, and vendors will be required if the bills are to be paid for the staff, facilities, and equipment needed to do the job of placement. Finally, the placement office of today and of the future must ensure its own viability in an academic environment that frequently does not understand the work that placement professionals do on behalf of their common clients, the students. The placement office, if it is to succeed, must be its own advocate and must be able to articulate its place in the university or college. By communicating what we can do for students and staff, we can partner with faculty, other student services, the development office, and so on to our mutual benefit and the benefit of our students.

## References

Breneman, D. W. *Guaranteed Student Loans: Great Success or Dismal Failure?* United Student Aid Funds, 1991.

College Placement Council. *1991 Career Planning and Placement Survey.* Bethlehem, Pa.: College Placement Council, 1991.

Commission on Professionals in Science and Technology. *Manpower Comments,* 1992, *29* (4), 1–2.

National Association of College and University Business Officers. *NACUBO Benchmarking Project Functional Manager Instructions for Collecting Benchmarking Data.* Washington, D.C.: National Association of College and University Business Officers, 1992.

Paquette, J. W. "Student Credentials: What Elements Are Really Essential?" *Journal of College Placement,* 1966, *26* (4), 35–44.

Powell, C. R., and Kirts, D. K. *Career Services Today: A Dynamic College Profession.* Bethlehem, Pa.: College Placement Council, 1980.

## Additional Resources

College Recruitment Data Base. *The Human Resource Information Network,* Executive Telecom System International, College Park North, 9585 Valparaiso Court, Indianapolis, IN 46268-1130.

DASIS, National Center for Computer Standards in Recruitment and Placement, 50 Lind Hall, Minneapolis, MN 55455.

kiNexus, 640 North LaSalle Street, Suite 560, Chicago, IL 60610.

National Association of College and University Business Officers, One DuPont Circle, Suite 510, Washington, DC 20036.

Peterson's Connexion, P.O. Box 2123, Princeton, NJ 08543.

*RICHARD A. STEWART is director of placement services at Purdue University, West Lafayette, Indiana. He is also president of the College Placement Council.*

*This chapter presents eight themes that constitute both a springboard for careful evaluation of current career counseling practices and a call to action for the career counseling profession.*

# Career Counseling: A Call to Action

*Mary J. Heppner, Joseph A. Johnston*

Career counseling services on most campuses are often given little prominence and are relegated to the least skilled counselors. If placed within a comprehensive counseling center, career services receive little attention. If housed in a center specifically designed for career services, they typically risk being understaffed, underfunded, and underused. While one could make a good case that career counseling is central to the mission of any college or university, that case has not been made with much success on most campuses. Too often career counseling centers do not have their vision communicated in a mission statement that can be a springboard to innovation and change.

The above remarks are not intended as criticism of the field but rather as commentary on the state of most career counseling operations, on most campuses, in the 1990s. As we approach the turn of the century, colleges and universities are being pressed to assert their role and mission, and to become much more accountable to their constituents. It seems a fitting time to examine the role of career counseling on campus and to rethink the manner in which it can emerge as a profession. In this chapter, eight themes are presented for careful consideration. Through self-study and examination of these critical themes, career centers can rightfully become a logical and significant part of the services and networks that colleges and universities must have to survive in hard economic times (Heppner and Johnston, 1986). While the number of themes is arbitrary, the eight areas covered provide beginning steps in examining ways of improving and enhancing career counseling services on our college and university campuses.

THEME 1. *Determine, prioritize, and promote the scope of services provided by the career counseling center and relate these to the missions of both the career center and the institution.*

Career services were once only placement services. The essential activity was a matching of graduates with employers. Today, the services increasingly include everything from recruitment to retention activities and then some. The career center affects recruitment efforts, for example, by serving as visible representation of the collective offerings of the institution. It affects financial aid efforts through job locator programs. It also enhances educational offerings through the provision of internships and cooperative education experiences and provides career information and counseling, preplacement services, and academic advising. It is fair to say that the career center could be involved wherever there is need for better understanding, interpretation, or utilization of the educational experience. However defined, the career center has, and should have, an evolving role.

A vision of what can or should be a part of the mission of a career center is best achieved by considering how it conforms with the larger mission of the college or university. For example, if the institutional mission calls for recruitment as a priority, and the career center is to be a part of that effort, then resources must be committed. What *can* be part of the career center mission is apt to be too narrow or too broad to be handled well without a careful scrutiny of functions. Staffing and the commitment of other resources require prioritizing; otherwise burnout and compromise become the norm. With a consensus about what will be emphasized in the mission, it will also be easier to promote the center.

A clear mission statement helps promote an appropriate tension between maintenance of good programs and the need to move ahead with new programs. It is easy, however, to agree on a mission statement and then forget it. It should evolve with the changing role of the higher education institution, and in today's world that evolution implies the necessity of reexamination on a fairly regular basis. Some examples can help clarify this point.

One college grappled with its decreasing enrollments by emphasizing its graduate programs. When that happened, the career center reexamined its programs for helping students find appropriate graduate school options. It added new computerized programs to help students practice graduate school admissions tests and increased its emphasis on preparing students for graduate school interviews as opposed to employment interviews. It deemphasized its recruitment of undergraduates.

In another example, a college took seriously the increasing number of adults coming to the college and opened the career counseling center during evenings and staffed it with adults who had recently returned to college. Since new resources were not available for this new program, the college had to reprioritize what was important as part of the mission.

A changing or dynamic mission requires an equally dynamic promotional program that keeps the institution and the patrons informed of changes. It is easy to assume that everyone is aware of changes, but in fact many students, and especially faculty, base their impressions of the career counseling center on old data. For example, when a center decides to emphasize internships or part-time employment opportunities—the current high-profile programs of the 1990s—it needs to promote those ideas among all of its constituents, many of whom will be new to the campus every semester. It is important to develop effective, regular avenues of communication: face-to-face interaction as well as the typical means of newsletters, posters, classroom postings, and campus mailings.

Prioritization of programs can have numerous benefits. If done in an appropriate manner, it can help staff focus their energies. It can be a way of recognizing the efforts of those who are attending to the programs that have been prioritized. It can also provide a formal way of recognizing the termination of a program. There is sometimes a need to end or deemphasize a program that can no longer be a priority. Staff can be recognized for past programmatic efforts yet be encouraged to let go of obsolete offerings and then formally reprioritize their efforts.

The promotion of programs can have side benefits. All staff members want to feel that their efforts make a difference, and seeing their programs promoted adds to that feeling. When their programs are viewed as contributing to the broader mission of the institution, that too increases their feelings of worth and reinforces the idea that the support mission of the center is important to the main mission of the institution. The joint sponsorship of programs with academic units achieves these ends as well, and even though joint efforts of this kind are often difficult to set up, they add considerably in subtle ways to the promotion of the center and its programs.

THEME 2. *Design the career counseling center to reflect what is current and successful practice in settings where the mission is primarily oriented toward information and service.*

There are numerous practices that should influence the design of career counseling centers. While businesses have stronger financial investments and better resources to ensure that their practices are appropriate, it is just good sense to take advantage of what businesspeople know and are doing. These practices can be incorporated into the arena of career counseling in at least three ways: in the design of the center, in the consideration of the services provided, and in the careful and continual analysis of the ways in which the services are provided. Since much of what is to be done in the coming century is likely to be different from current practices, these considerations demand constant reexamination. However, some of these practices are so successful and well established in business that they should be implemented immediately in education circles. Hence, we discuss here some of the ideas that should be common practice and reflect on ways to act on ideas as they emerge.

**Atmosphere.** If the function of the center is primarily to serve students, design it to reflect what makes them comfortable. Informality tends to make students more comfortable. Music helps. Good signage helps. Location helps. An atmosphere that promotes self-exploration helps. Staff members who make finding things simple and quick help. A casual drop-in arrangement where others can be seen engaged in exploration helps. A multimedia, technologically sophisticated component brings credibility and appeal to the center.

It may be necessary to visit McDonald's, Disneyland, video arcades, and dormitory rooms, and to watch television advertisements, "MTV," telephone company promotions, and the like, to see what, from the standpoint of business, is capturing the attention of youth in this country. An education mission may call for a tempering of that commercialism, and it is important to give the mission statement a meaningful educational twist or spin, but the message should be exploited for our purposes: Marketing is important and necessary if we are to reach students.

Students are not all alike, and an atmosphere that makes some students comfortable is not what will draw others in for services. McDonald's, for example, creates many atmospheres within the same building and even allows patrons to get services without entering the building. A career center needs to do the same. The atmosphere needs to reflect what makes most students comfortable and still provide opportunities for others to find ways to use the career center. Some students are not motivated to do things in the way in which institutions prescribe or at the time that is thought to be most appropriate. The atmosphere and even the hours of the center should reflect an awareness of what is known about the student clientele: age, sex, marital status, ethnicity, comfort with academia, and the like.

**Staffing.** A staffing pattern that is based on the value of self-help and other approaches to learning can dramatically change and revitalize a career center. Some services are better provided in a mode that allows and encourages people to do things for themselves. Many of the services of a career center fit well within that framework. Basic career information and popular resources, for example, properly displayed and easily accessible, can encourage students to gather information on their own. Answering of repetitive questions can demean and defeat a professional staff member. Further, there is evidence that many people prefer to help themselves and will do so if the process is made simple. It is wise to "learn to do things on your own," especially if "next time you'll have to do it on your own." If students learn to do it on their own in college, a purported objective for the graduate, this kind of exploration will contribute to their sense of self-sufficiency.

The real difficulty with center staffing may come from an unwillingness or an inability of staff members to give up the information-providing role. For many, this role is rewarding, and they are good at it. But they will be good at other things too, and these other talents and skills can emerge as part of a new role for them as professionals. The sole task of giving information is not sufficient for an individual who is paid as a professional. Not only do many students prefer to acquire information on their own, but if they need help finding it, they often prefer to receive help from a peer rather than a professional.

**Helping.** Peers can provide a substantial portion of the services requested by students. This fact has been known for some time, yet few centers make optimal use of peers. Peers can not only provide these services, but enjoy and learn from the process, and, candidly, they provide some services far better than a professional staff can. Much of this peer advantage stems from the obvious preference of adolescents to take advice from peers during this period of their lives. But peer staff members do not negate the impact and input of the professional staff. In many ways, they enhance that role and bring it more in line with what professionals have been trained to do.

The presence of peers increases the comfort and credibility of the center and the importance of the professional. Peer staff need professional staff who identify with them and their training. Those professionals must be good at communicating with paraprofessionals, putting theory into practice, simplifying the career development process, and motivating, supervising, and leading a diverse and challenging group of helpers. Since turnover is a fact of life in a student staff, recruitment and training are ongoing activities. But the effort, if sustained, is exceptionally rewarding in terms of activity, quality of service, and, eventually, more appropriate use of the professional staff. Peers, and the staff who train and support them, are the building blocks of an effective career counseling center in the 1990s.

If a peer staff is so important and so obvious, why have more centers not committed to a staffing pattern that includes peers? There are probably numerous reasons. First, the usual staffing commitment is a director and possibly a secretary or assistant director. These are vital positions, and together they can attend to an impressive array of tasks. In fact, for accountability purposes, they may be essential. No one would question whether they can be kept busy. Typically, they can be so busy that they never again see the forest through the trees. If true to the pattern, they become exhausted and in a few years seek promotion or a new position where the routines are less stressful. Second, there may be reservations about what a peer staff can do. With limited monies, a paraprofessional program represents a sizable investment. It often means trading a full-time professional line—that next person who might help provide relief to an already overworked staff—for a major conversion of the center to accommodate and train a critical mass of youthful specialists. Further, once the staff realizes its potential, much of the day-to-day operation should be given over to them. That may make some professionals uncomfortable, especially if they are accustomed to running things themselves. And, frankly, many professionals simply prefer doing all of the work themselves. When that is the case, this change in staffing pattern is nearly impossible. A third reason, then, that centers have not incorporated a peer staff is that many have gone too long and done too well without paraprofessionals. To be sure, when their operations were mostly oriented toward placement, the need and appeal of paraprofessionals was less an issue. The management of a routine placement operation without them was not a big loss, and in fact, some could argue, it would have been inappropriate. But times have changed, and there is a need for change in staffing patterns.

To understand the consequences of a major commitment to a peer specialist program, we need only imagine that instead of using monies for the next professional staff addition—say, the third or fourth staff member on the team—a center committed these monies to the hiring of twenty-five students from the campus, with each paid about $1,000 to work in the center twelve hours per week for two semesters. Even though the full-time staff would have to commit a major share of their time to train this group, the paraprofessionals would be available for 250 to 300 hours of staff time each week, doing some things more effectively and appropriately than the professionals! Again, freeing the professionals to do other things! The possibilities are unlimited.

A paraprofessional staff arrangement has its strengths, but it also has its liabilities. Since the liabilities emerge first, many centers drop the program before appreciating the benefits. Further, if the early staffing pattern does not include paraprofessionals, it may be more difficult to incorporate them later. A brief look at one center's successful experience with paraprofessionals illustrates some of the essential elements that have kept the peer staff in place.

The career center at the University of Missouri, Columbia, has had a paraprofessional program since its inception some twenty years ago (Johnston and Hansen, 1981). The program emerged for three major reasons: First, several people believed strongly in a peer helping model; second, several people were good at the training and supervision of undergraduates; and, third, there was a need to provide a kind of career service to the campus that was not being provided by the existing professional staff. A fourth reason, though not clearly essential, was that the need emerged but not the budget; hence, it was initially a volunteer staffing arrangement that answered a need without costing much money. Today the paraprofessionals are all paid.

In the early years of operation, attention was drawn to what peers could not do well or appropriately: interpret career tests, provide professional counseling, and relate to faculty or staff who had different expectations about the role of paraprofessionals as providers of services. With training, supervised experience, outreach activities in classes, faculty dialogues and interactions with well-trained peers, good lines of referral for situations that peers were not comfortable handling, and other, less formal activities, attention began to shift away from what peers do not do well to what they do best: bring students to the center, create an inviting environment for their colleagues, present and represent the center in classes and in their living units, and generally make the career center a student center. The training involved in making them an important influence is well documented elsewhere (Hansen and Johnston, 1986). What is important here is that, initially, there was considerable resistance to the program and only a persistent effort made obvious what it had to offer. Too often the commitment to stay the course is not sufficient, and the center never sees the real benefits of this staffing model.

A careful analysis of the nature of the services to be provided should make obvious the need for paraprofessionals. A successful business with goods or services that can be provided with minimal assistance to consumers would opt to hire associates or clerks, not increase the number of managers.

All staff need training for the services that they provide. Paraprofessionals need constant training and supervision. However, once the nature of the services is closely examined, it is clear that a center committed to providing a broad array of programs and to reaching large numbers of students is better served with a staffing pattern that includes paraprofessionals.

THEME 3. *Build the career counseling center on solid philosophical and psychological bases.*

In the hustle of day-to-day operations, it may be difficult to stop and consider the whys and the wherefores of a career center. Numerous philosophical questions arise daily. For example, are the services designed for all students or only for those who feel that they need them? Should they be part and parcel of curriculum offerings, or can they be independent of the academic curriculum? Should the center be academically oriented, or a support service, or a combination of both? Should peers be incorporated into the center? Can students be thought of as independent adults who can be expected to find themselves on their own? Are centers obligated to find and help those who do not help themselves?

These are a sample of questions that eventually will confront the staff; the way in which they are answered will direct the nature of nearly all of the activity and effort of the center. It is important to build on the answers to these and similar questions.

There are also similar psychological questions: How do students best learn or make decisions? How are they motivated? How and when do they best process information? How do they learn about their interests, skills, values, and so on and come to accept them and represent them to others? Who and what are the most important influences in career decisions, and how are they best brought to bear on decisions? What about readiness for learning? What has meaning for students? What belongs in a set of criteria for happiness? What do students need to learn about leisure? How do career counseling staff simulate or create real-life experiences for them?

These are only a few of the questions that require familiarity with good psychological theory. Theory helps to focus practice. If articulated well, it can help staff understand the why of their efforts and it can help organize all of the center's activity. Theory also can make easier the articulation of roles and functions and help staff and patrons see how each activity fits into the bigger picture.

As an illustration of how philosophical and psychological theory can determine practice, consider the case of one career counseling center that adopted Holland's (1992) theory of how people make career choices and combined it with the psychological notion that college students can and should learn how to help themselves. The center and its activities can be assessed in terms of at least these two theoretical bases. Specifically, we can ask how well each activity in the center contributes to an expansion of a student's thinking or implementation of what is needed to make good choices. Do people know themselves and the world of work well enough to implement the theory for themselves?

Holland's theory emphasizes the fit between personality type and work environments. The theory proposes that there are six types of personalities and work environments: realistic, investigative, artistic, social, enterprising, and conventional. It is based on the proposition that people search for environments that allow them to use their abilities and to express their values and interests. Generally, the theory contends that individuals are happier and more satisfied if there is compatibility or fit between their personality type and their chosen environment.

To reflect this theory, the center is divided into six personality areas, similar to the six types and environments described in Holland's theory. These are color coded to help the center's clients find material related to their types and environments. Occupational information is arranged in a similar fashion, so the storage and subsequent exploration of information reinforce the theory. To encourage self-exploration, open tubs, rather than file cabinets, are used for the display of information. Paraprofessionals trained to understand and articulate the theory in practical terms are part of the staff, since college students learn so well from peers. Wall pictures visually represent the theory by depicting the six personality types. The self-assessment instruments available reinforce the students' characterization of themselves in terms of Holland's typology. As much as possible, these are self-directed instruments. Group activities are designed with the subtle, if not overt, objective of having students learn something about themselves in terms of the career choice model. In choosing books, printed materials, and computerized programs for self-exploration, the staff considered how well these materials promote an understanding of the ideas behind the theory and how well they lend themselves to self-exploration. A center built on solid theoretical ideas has far more credibility with students and the academic community in general; staff are also better able to choose and evaluate resources and programs.

THEME 4. *Carefully design interventions to match the developmental needs of the clientele.*

> When arriving for her first career counseling intake appointment, Regina told her intake worker that she needed "someone with experience who can tell me what I should be." When the intake worker described the variety of options available to her, Regina opted for an interest inventory, because a friend in the residence hall had taken one and it had "told her to become an accountant and that was working out really well for her." Regina was feeling increasingly anxious about her indecision. She felt that everyone else in her classes knew exactly what they were going to do for the rest of their lives, and she wanted to know that too.

> Chuck's dad had insisted that he make an appointment for counseling in order to "stop drifting and get something decided about your career plans." Chuck was a business major but was feeling very ambivalent about narrowing his occupational choices any further. He had talked to a lot of his professors and they all seemed to have very different perspectives. Chuck was just beginning to appreciate the ramifications of his decisions. He was feeling a lot of anxiety and had a desire to put off making a decision as long as possible.

Career counselors who help students similar to Regina and Chuck can benefit greatly from the research of developmental theorists in designing and implementing their own career counseling services. Developmental theorists have identified important tasks for individuals to master at various levels. Perry (1970), for example, has provided a useful framework for examining developmental needs. But because his research subjects were primarily male, it is important to consider as well the work of Belenky, Clinchy, Goldberger, and Tarule (1986). They found that while the broad categories of developmental change are similar for males and females, there are differences between men's and women's views of knowledge (how they know), authority, and truth. Kurfiss (1988) integrated the work of these two research groups (Perry and Belenky and colleagues) into the following categories: Level 1 is dualism and received knowledge, level 2 is multiplicity and subjective knowledge, level 3 is relativism and procedural knowledge, and level 4 is commitment in relativism and constructed knowledge. While a description of these stages is beyond the scope of this chapter, a rudimentary application of the model to the lives of Regina and Chuck at least highlights the importance of understanding developmental levels in clients.

Regina is a first-year college student who is probably at level 1 in her development. Level 1 is characterized by a belief that there is a right answer and probably only one right answer to a career dilemma. Level 1 thinkers view authorities (for example, career counselors) as sources of these right answers, available for the asking. Belenky, Clinchy, Goldberger, and Tarule (1986) refer to this as a belief in "received knowledge." At this level, it is difficult for the client to see that there are potentially many satisfying career choices and that once a career choice is made, the likelihood that it will be changed is great. Tasks for the counselor at this stage may consist of helping Regina dispel mistaken notions such as that authorities and tests represent knowledge superior to her own, that there is one right career field for her, and that once made, this choice is irreversible. A problem at this stage is that students often make premature career decisions in order to feel more secure. The counselor may need to provide support and structure so that Regina understands that although she may not have the answer now, exploration will lead her to a sound career decision.

In contrast, Chuck is beginning to experience level 2 conflicts. Unlike Regina, he is beginning to realize the complexity of his choices, that there is not one right answer, and that even respected authorities disagree in their perspectives. Chuck is at a stage in which he needs to start developing trust in his own inner voice, but he feels as though he has little experience at this task. His anxiety at this stage may keep him from action. Chuck's counselor has the challenge of working with him at a very critical point in his development. This is a stage where Chuck will be struggling to become more aware of what he thinks, of his own needs and interests. While at times it might feel overwhelming to make career decisions at this level, Chuck may be helped by seeing this as a lifelong process, not one discrete decision. The counselor can help Chuck clarify his own values and affirm his own voice.

These developmental theories of Perry (1970) and Belenky, Clinchy, Goldberger, and Tarule (1986) provide helpful information with which to tailor career interventions. Another rich area of theory and research that has developed in the last two decades is adult development and the tasks and life stages that are critical to the career development of adults. Theorists such as Jung (1961), Buhler and Massarik (1968), Erikson (1950), Havinghurst (1948), and Sanford (1966) have provided a rich base for the adult development research and theories of Levinson (1978), Gould (1972), Sheehy (1974), Valliant (1971), and Neugarten (1966). On the whole, this work can help career counselors better understand the developmental stages or tasks as well as the feelings of adults who come in for career counseling. With this understanding, counselors are better equipped to design appropriate and effective interventions.

THEME 5. *Develop a sophisticated diagnostic system for providing services.*

Assessment has been at the heart of vocational psychology from its beginning in the early 1900s. Parsons (1909) emphasized the importance of knowing oneself as the first step in a career planning process. Vocational psychologists down through the century have been at the forefront of the development and refinement of psychometric instruments that help individuals understand more about their interests, values, and skills. The field, however, has not focused as much attention on individual differences among clients who come in for career counseling services (Fretz, 1981). Too often, all clients who come in for career counseling are treated the same, with little attention paid to how each individual's needs and circumstances are unique. A greater number of writers are addressing this issue of individual differences in the professional literature (Fuqua and Hartman, 1982), however; researchers are beginning to examine different subtypes of undecided students (Larson, Heppner, Ham, and Dugan, 1988) and to distinguish between undecided and indecisive students (Fuqua and Hartman, 1983). Nevertheless, while this dialogue is taking place in the professional literature, there is little evidence that differen-tial diagnosis is occurring in practice. As Fuqua and Hartman (1983) have argued, the student who comes in for career counseling is quite likely to receive traditional career services, for instance, interest testing and occupational resource materials. Although this approach may work well with some indviduals, we must become more sophisticated in our diagnostic techniques  in order to meet the career counseling needs of all individuals who seek our services.

The following two case examples highlight the importance of differential diagnosis:

John came in for a career counseling appointment at the beginning of his sophomore year. He had been in college for over a year and was having difficulty deciding on what major and eventual occupation he wanted to pursue. He was considering both business and law but was not sure which would be the best fit for him. His parents were supportive and just wanted him to be happy. John was doing well academically and liked school, but he wanted to find out more about law and business and perhaps even some other occupations that he had not thought of pursuing.

Susan came in for a career counseling appointment at the beginning of her sophomore year. She had been in college for over a year and was having difficulty deciding on what major and eventual occupation she wanted to pursue. Susan appeared anxious and expressed that she has always had difficulty "making up my mind about a lot of things—and this is no exception." She hoped that the career counselor would be able to tell her which occupation she should pursue. She had been referred to career counseling by her therapist, who was working with her on a variety of issues stemming from her upbringing in an alcoholic family.

John and Susan are coming to career counseling with a lot of similarities: they are both traditional age college students, in the beginning of their sophomore year, who are feeling the need to have clearer ideas about their career directions. John fits the profile of a typical undecided student who needs more information in order to make a good career decision (Salomone, ıf his counselor works with him using traditional career counseling ͡ͅchniques, which might include interest testing and occupational information, research indicates that this will likely be an effective and satisfying intervention. If Susan is provided the same services, the prediction of efficacy and satisfaction is not nearly so promising.

As McAuliffe (1991) has argued, individuals like Susan, who have personal emotional barriers to decision making, may not benefit from traditional information-oriented interventions. Rather, it may be most effective to help Susan understand more about the barriers that she is experiencing. Susan fits the profile of the indecisive student. This indecisiveness is usually characterized by extreme anxiety, lack of separation from parents, and global inability in decision making (Fuqua and Hartman, 1983; Lopez and Andrews, 1987; Salomone, 1982).

In the past thirteen years, a number of assessment measures have been developed to help clients understand more about the internal and external barriers that they may experience when making career decisions. We review four of these instruments and discuss how the information from them can be used to help target interventions in the career planning process:

*My Vocational Situation.* This diagnostic instrument (Holland, Diager, and Power, 1980), short and easily scored, assesses problems with career development in three areas: vocational identity (VI) refers to "the procession of a clear and stable picture of one's goals, interests, personality, and talents" (Holland, Diager, and Power, 1980, p. 1). The VI scale is composed of eighteen true-false items; the range of VI scores is 0–18, with 18 indicating the strongest sense of vocational identity. The barriers scale and the occupational information scale consist of four yes-no items.

*Career Transitions Inventory.* This inventory (M. Heppner, 1991) is a forty-five-item Likert-type instrument designed to assess an individual's internal process variables that may serve as strengths or barriers when making a career transition. The responses to the items range between 1 (strongly agree) and 6 (strongly disagree). The total score range is between 112 and 254. Factor-analysis studies revealed five items: career motivation (readiness), self-efficacy (confidence), social support (support), internal/external (control), and self versus relational focus (independence-interdependence). High scores are positive and indicate that the person perceives himself or herself to be doing well in that area; low scores indicate barriers.

*Career Beliefs Inventory.* This tool (Krumboltz, 1991) is designed to measure "beliefs that block people from achieving their career goals" (Krumboltz, 1991, p. 1). The inventory contains ninety-six items, answered on a 5-point rating scale from "strongly agree" to "strongly disagree." It yields twenty-five scales and an administrative index to estimate response accuracy. The twenty-five scales are organized under five headings: "My Current Career Situation," "What Seems Necessary for My Happiness," "Factors That Influence My Decisions," "Changes I Am Willing to Make," and "Effort I Am

Willing to Initiate." The inventory is best described by its creator, John D. Krumboltz (1991, p. 1): "The fundamental premise upon which the CBI is based is that people make a number of assumptions and generalizations about themselves and the work world based on their limited experiences. Whether accurate or not, these assumptions affect the way people behave. If people believe something is true, they act as if it is true. What appears to be inappropriate or self-defeating behavior may become understandable when one discovers the assumptions and beliefs on which each person operates."

*Hope Scale.* This scale (Snyder and others, 1991) is a twelve-item inventory containing eight hope items and four distracters. Four of the hope items measure a construct called agency; the other four measure pathways. The agency items are constructed to measure one's past, present, and future sense of goal-related determination. The following is an example of an item on this scale: "I meet the goals that I set for myself." The four pathways items refer to a person's perceived level of ability to think of ways to proceed even if obstacles are present. The following is an example of a pathways item: "I can think of many ways to get out of a jam." While this instrument has been primarily used in medically related research, the construct of hope also seems to be relevant to individuals who are attempting to make important life and career decisions.

These four examples of diagnostic instruments are recommended to help career counselors diagnose individuals who come in for career counseling, and to more fully understand the personality factors and barriers that these individuals may be experiencing as they pursue either first occupations or transitions in later life. Information gained from such assessments can greatly aid the counselor in developing targeted interventions. If, for example, individuals have faulty belief systems as measured by the Career Beliefs Inventory, if their self-efficacy about their ability to make the career change is low as measured by the Career Transitions Inventory, if they have unclear vocational identities as measured by My Vocational Situation, and if they perceive themselves as having few pathways as measured by the Hope Scale, these pieces of information can be critically important in developing counseling goals and interventions. The strength of these instruments is that they help both client and counselor assess the more internal dynamic variables that often serve as barriers to individuals in the career planning and career change process.

THEME 6. *Provide continual training for staff and build a strong network with other professionals on campus and across the nation.*

Career counseling is a rapidly changing field, and to be effective, one must find ways to keep in touch with the constant flow of new ideas. For example, of the four assessment instruments reviewed above, three were developed in the last five years, and all four are still being validated in significant ways. If an individual completed his or her master's degree only five years ago, most of these instruments would not have been mentioned in the curriculum. How to stay current is a problem, but one must recognize the importance of keeping abreast of the latest trends and innovations and consider various ways to achieve this goal.

Proper training begins with good attitudes. Training needs to be viewed as ongoing and applicable to the job. As is the case with career planning, timing is everything. Hence, to be effective, training must be seen as ongoing activity emerging from day-to-day practice. When staff see training as essential to greater effectiveness in their work, they are apt to participate with a sense of purpose.

With a staff of no more than three or four professionals, who often have quite different responsibilities, it is important to find ways to stay in touch with others doing similar things at different places. Books, journals, newsletters, conventions, teleconferences, electronic mail, and even telephone calls are good ways. If expenses are at issue, most centers can find colleagues doing similar things at neighboring institutions. For the cost of a luncheon, there can be meaningful exchanges of ideas without the presence of paid experts. Occasionally, an outside speaker or consultant is appropriate, but this individual is probably most effective when brought in to address a specific concern that has emerged from practice within the center.

Some guidelines for training might be useful. Build training around practice. Pay close attention to needs that emerge from the staff. Time the training to be an appropriate response to a staff need. Make training fun and rewarding. Constantly refer to the importance and outcomes of training. Invest in it. Expect it to pay dividends. Provide opportunities for staff to talk about it, and, as appropriate, make them trainers too. Career planning is a high-burnout area, and staff need to feel appreciated for the way in which they do things according to plan and for finding new ways to do things as well. An investment in training is one way to express that appreciation.

A final thought about the place of training: Expect turnover or burnout in two to three years if the staff members do not see ways to change, grow, or improve what they are doing. In fact, plan for turnover if staff performance does not evolve. The performance of largely repetitive activities, without change, quickly leads to staff indifference. Such an attitude can be avoided with a viable, ongoing training program.

THEME 7. *Attend to the increasing multicultural diversity of the student population.*

The population demographics of students on college campuses is changing dramatically, and these changes will continue to increase into the next century. Previously underrepresented groups are attending colleges and universities in record numbers. These figures reflect not only national demographic changes but also a growing awareness of past discrimination and more sophisticated attempts at remedying the problem of underrepresentation. For career counselors, these changes translate to an obligation to evaluate all aspects of service provision in order to ensure that the needs of multiracial and multiethnic groups are appropriately addressed in their career centers. This evaluation must include an examination of our theories, our assessment tools, our occupational information, the training of our staff, the atmosphere of our centers, and the manner in which we provide services. For years, most centers have tried to foster nondiscrimination, that is, to ensure that all students are treated equally. There is now a growing awareness of the need to go much further than equal services. We need to examine those services and determine how appropriate they are in relation to the diverse cultural backgrounds of many of our students.

The underutilization of all types of counseling services by underrepresented groups has been well documented (Brown, Brooks, and Associates, 1990). It has also been well documented that the termination rate after one counseling session for underrepresented group members is significantly higher than for majority group members (Sue and Sue, 1991). Clearly, our delivery systems have not been very successful in reaching underrepresented groups, and when these groups have been reached, our centers have not been very effective in providing ongoing services. In the last decade, much attention was given in professional journals to the task of delineating the problem. Now we must assess the entire span of our operations with the aim of increasing our effectiveness in serving underrepresented individuals. The following ten recommendations are offered as guides to this examination:

*Modify existing theories of career development to take into account the level of racial identity development.* Most of the career theories that are in use today were developed forty years ago. While that is impressive in terms of the theories' usefulness over time, we must keep in mind that these theories were largely developed with white (and in most cases male) college students as the research subjects. With the increasing diversity of our students, there is a need to examine, and in some cases modify, those theories to be more inclusive and helpful to the populations actually being served (Brown, Brooks, and Associates, 1990).

Parham and Helms's (1981) research on the issue of black racial identity development offers much to the informed modification of career theory. They have documented that minority group members go through different stages in their racial identity formation. These stages (preencounter, encounter, immersion, and internalization) relate to how the individual views himself or herself as a racial being. If an individual, for example, is at the encounter stage of identity formation, which is a period often triggered by an event (overt racism) that shakes the person's previous worldview and promotes very negative feelings toward whites and very positive feelings toward his or her own race, this may directly affect how the individual goes about the tasks and activities of career development (Super, 1980). Specifically, at the encounter stage of identity formation, the individual may limit himself or herself to careers that do not entail interaction with the majority population. This example highlights the need to examine all of the career development theories used and to modify them in a manner that is sensitive to developmental differences in racial identity formation.

*Choose assessment instruments that avoid bias and stereotypes.* In the career counseling profession, there has long been an awareness of the need to develop instruments that are free of bias and stereotypical presentations of information. Still, many of our instruments reflect the dominant culture of our society. Underrepresented group members may, through lack of exposure to various activities and occupations, score differently on interest assessments from members of the majority culture. One way of eliminating, or at least reducing, these differences is to use tools such as card sorts, where the career counselor can stay in constant contact with clients as they are doing the assessment. If a client is discarding many potential occupations, the counselor can then determine whether the client really dislikes the occupations or simply lacks information about them due to lack of role models or exposure to the activities. The counselor can encourage further exploration of a host of career fields that the client may never have considered, thus expanding his or her occupational options.

*Help the client examine society's stereotyping of different racial and ethnic groups and determine how much the client accepts the stereotypes.* Certain racial and ethnic groups have traditionally gone into certain occupations for a number of historical and societal reasons (Smith, 1983). Many times the structure of occupational opportunity has limited options for underrepresented groups. Career counselors must keep in mind that clients need help in examining their own acceptance of these stereotypical occupations, and help in determining the authenticity of their career decision-making process. There is certainly nothing wrong with pursuing occupations that have been culturally stereotyped (for example, Asians going into engineering and other technical fields); however, it may be important for the person to closely examine how these choices were made.

*Examine ethical issues involved in job interviewing.* For career counselors who also work with job placement or job interviewing, there are a variety of ethical issues related to helping a person from another ethnic or racial group conform to majority-style interviews. In many ways, interviewing requires all participants to put on an act. This requirement may hold even more strongly for minority group members. Some minority group members feel as though they have to "sell their soul to get the goal" of a job in a majority company. This "selling" may entail changing many aspects of their nonverbal behavior (eye contact), personality (overt enthusiasm), and clothing. It is important for career counselors to examine how to effectively handle these issues with minority clients.

*Expand outreach efforts.* Since members of underrepresented groups have, historically, not made use of counseling services to the same degree as majority students, it is critically important to expand outreach efforts to these groups. One avenue is to have career counselors offer programs and help with activities sponsored by various clubs and organizations serving minority students. The hiring of a culturally diverse professional and paraprofessional staff also is important in helping minority group clients feel comfortable about coming in for services. Demonstrating multicultural sensitivity in the choice of artwork and magazines displayed in the career offices is a little thing, but it can mean a lot to a minority person coming into a new setting.

*Develop self-efficacy through experiential learning activities.* Although the cultural diversity of students is increasing at colleges and universities, the completion rate of minority groups still remains considerably lower than that of the majority population. While there are many reasons for this difference, the inability to see oneself actually succeeding in a chosen occupational role may be a factor. As career counseling professionals, we know that a primary vehicle for improving one's self-efficacy in a given field is to actually work in the field and have successful experiences. The whole arena of experiential learning has great potential for influencing the self-efficacy of underrepresented groups. Internships, cooperative education programs, volunteer work, and career-related part-time jobs all offer the potential to increase a minority person's belief in his or her own ability to perform in a professional career role. These options need to be expanded and promoted with minority group members.

*Examine the role of career counselor as authority.* As career counselors, we need to be aware that some cultural groups look to us as authority figures and give us much more control than most of us can comfortably assume. Even more so than the majority students who want us to "tell them what to be," some cultures place a great emphasis on the wisdom of professionals and the wisdom of those older than oneself (Sue and Sue, 1991). How the career counselor handles this attribution of power is a personal decision, but one that needs to be carefully considered.

*Examine one's own cultural biases.* We also need to recognize that there are many cultural factors that affect a client's decision making regarding career choice. In white American culture, emphasis is placed on the concept of separation-individuation. It is seen as a sign of healthy developmental adjustment for a college student to separate from his or her family of origin and begin to make important life decisions independently. For culturally diverse clients, this same emphasis may not be meaningful (Sue and Sue, 1991). When we hear an Asian junior talk about needing to discuss a change of career emphasis with his family, we need to be sensitive to this cultural difference and not assume that the person is having difficulty with a basic developmental task of college students. This is but one example of a host of cultural differences that can affect career counseling with culturally diverse clients. It is our professional responsibility to be aware of the culture-based beliefs and values of our clients.

*Consider the client's level of acculturation.* Research on the issue of directive versus nondirective counseling styles with culturally diverse clients has only recently begun but is already challenging the sweeping generalizations in the professional literature indicating that all nonmajority clients prefer a very directive, task-oriented style. Some of this new research points to the need to determine the level of acculturation of the client. That is, the research findings indicate that the more acculturated minority clients are in relation to the majority culture, the more likely they are to desire less direction and a more insight-oriented approach in the counseling that they receive. Although research on this topic is in its infancy, the importance of matching one's style to the preferred style of the client must be recognized if the counselor is to effectively meet the client's career planning needs.

*Become the client's advocate.* Since discrimination on the bases of race, disability, affectional preference, gender, and the like still exists, it is important that career professionals become advocates for their clients as they face possible bias and discrimination in their pursuit of careers (Sue and Sue, 1991). The ability to recognize and address overt and subtle discrimination is an important life skill for the culturally diverse client.

THEME 8. *Engage in practice that is guided by research, and conduct research that is guided by practice.*

Two important parts of what make career counseling a profession are its firm grounding in scientific theory and continued reliance on data-based research to guide practice. Unfortunately, these critical elements of the profession are not evident in some career development settings. There appears to be a widening gap between the professionals interested in career-related research and those interested in career-related practice. Although many of the training programs for career professionals espouse the importance of the "scientist-practitioner model" (Raimy, 1950), many professionals experience difficulty in trying to make this philosophy work. In order to maintain professionalism and provide the most effective services to clients, it is critical for practice to be guided by research and for career services to be based on research that is guided by practice.

There are a number of reasons that this marriage of science and practice is difficult. These have been well documented in the professional literature (see P. Heppner and others, 1992) and include such factors as the lack of models of this integration in our graduate training programs and curricula, the propensity of our journals to publish basic scientific research that has limited applicability to practice settings, the lack of dialogue between those who call themselves scientists and those who call themselves practitioners, the lack of support and resources for those who work in practice settings to conduct scientific research, and the personality differences between those career development professionals who pursue academic careers and those who pursue practice-based careers.

It is imperative that we overcome these problems in order to provide the highest quality service and research to the career development field. The following five recommendations for practice settings may help to bridge the gap between science and practice.

*Make a regular practice of using professional journals to guide decision making about clinical practice.* There is, for example, a growing body of knowledge related to the counseling of undecided college students (Larson, Heppner, Ham, and Dugan, 1988; Salomone, 1982). The research indicates that the term *undecided* does not describe a homogeneous group of students. Rather, there are various subtypes of undecided students with quite different personality characteristics. The research has clear implications for practitioners. We need to be able to identify the type of undecided student with whom we are working and then develop appropriate interventions based on that type. This is but one example of the many ways in which research can help practitioners develop more effective interventions. As we counsel clients and as we train the next generation of career counselors, using the scientific base provided by our professional journals, it is essential that we provide the most effective services to our clients.

*Develop liaisons with faculty members who are interested in career-related research.* Career counseling centers are always attempting, often quite unsuccessfully, to get more input from faculty members. Often, faculty members are asked to devote time to activities for which they will not be supported by their home departments. But most faculty are interested in conducting research and would welcome the opportunity to have dialogue with career practitioners about the issues they encounter in their day-to-day work with career clients. These types of liaisons can be very beneficial to the faculty member as well as to the practitioner.

*Develop research teams of practitioners and faculty.* It is well known that many practitioners choose to pursue the practice side of the profession because of their personality traits (Holland, 1985). Many find the independent and autonomous role of the scientist undesirable. The purpose of research teams is to integrate diverse expertise from both practice and science, and to do it in a more social and less isolating manner than characterizes most research efforts.

*Encourage the use of scientific thinking in clinical practice.* When engaged in career counseling, practitioners should be encouraged to use the skills of case conceptualization and hypothesis making and testing with their clients. Intuition is an important component of clinical work. Practitioners should have hunches. These hunches are really hypotheses, from a scientific perspective. They can be used to guide counseling and intervention strategies with clients.

*Make use of more qualitative and single-subject research designs.* Part of the complaint that practitioners have long had about the type of research produced and published in our professional journals is that it is conducted in a manner that does not lead to useful findings and implications for the practitioner. This situation may be a result of the goal of trying to gain professional credibility by using the empirical, quantitative research methods of the "hard sciences" (P. Heppner and others, 1992). Recently, career counseling professionals have recognized the importance of using qualitative methodologies as well. Also, much work has been done to improve these qualitative methodologies. They have become much more rigorous and sophisticated and, as such, are more resistant to threats to internal validity (P. Heppner, Kivlighan, and Wampold, 1991). This new emphasis on methodologies such as single-subject process research, needs assessments, and interview protocols may eventually produce more useful information for the practitioner.

These five recommendations are aimed at helping practitioners think about how they can bridge the gap between science and practice. But we also must examine the ways in which researchers can produce investigations that are more relevant to practitioners. With both sides working harder to save this marriage, there can be both better quality research and more effective service for clients.

## Conclusion

It is the purpose of this chapter to encourage counselors' self-study and reflection in the career development area. The eight themes presented here are intended as a springboard for careful evaluation of a variety of aspects of career counseling practices. They are also intended as a call to action, because only through action can we effect the types of radical changes needed to bring career centers to the center of campus life. The mission is too important to be on the periphery. The goals are too essential to be held back by underfunded, understaffed operations. The clientele of the twenty-first century will bring with them more diverse needs for career services than perhaps ever before confronted by career counselors. Only through self-examination and change can we meet the challenge.

## References

Belenky, M. F., Clinchy, B. M., Goldberger, N. R., and Tarule, J. M. *Women's Ways of Knowing: The Development of Self, Voice, and Mind.* New York: Basic Books, 1986.

Brown, D., Brooks, L., and Associates. *Career Choice and Development: Applying Contemporary Theories to Practice.* (2nd ed.) San Francisco: Jossey-Bass, 1990.

Buhler, C., and Massarik, F. *The Course of Human Life.* New York: Springer, 1968.

Erickson, E. H. *Childhood and Society.* New York: Norton, 1950.

Fretz, B. "Evaluation Career Interventions." *Journal of Counseling Psychology,* 1981, *28,* 77–90.

Fuqua, D. R., and Hartman, B. W. "Differential Diagnosis and Treatment of Career Indecision." Paper presented at the annual meeting of the American Educational Research Association, Montreal, Canada, Apr. 1982.

Fuqua, D. R., and Hartman, B. W. "Differential Diagnosis and Treatment of Career Indecision." *Personnel and Guidance Journal,* 1983, *62,* 27–29.

Gould, R. L. "The Phases of Adult Life: A Study in Developmental Psychology." *American Journal of Psychiatry,* 1972, *5,* 521–531.

Hansen, R. N., and Johnston, M. C. "College Students as Paraprofessional Career Specialists." *Journal of Career Development,* 1986, *13* (1), 18–29.

Havinghurst, R. J. *Developmental Tasks and Education.* New York: McKay, 1948.

Heppner, M. J. "The Career Transitions Inventory (CTI)." Unpublished manuscript, Department of Psychology, University of Missouri, 1991.

Heppner, M. J., and Johnston, J. A. "Career Centers: A Continually Expanding Role." *Journal of Career Development,* 1986, *13* (1), 5–8.

Heppner, P. P., Carter, J. A., Claiborn, C. D., Brooks, L., Gelso, C., Fassinger, R. E., Holloway, E. L., Stone, G. L., Wampold, B. E., and Galassi, J. P. "A Proposal to Integrate Science and Practice in Counseling Psychology." *Counseling Psychologist,* 1992, *20,* 107–122.

Heppner, P. P., Kivlighan, D. M., and Wampold, B. E. *Research Design in Counseling.* Pacific Grove, Calif.: Brooks/Cole, 1991.

Holland, J. L. *Making Vocational Choices: A Theory of Vocational Personalities and Work Environments.* (2nd ed.) Odessa, Fla.: Psychological Assessment Resources, 1992.

Holland, J. L., Daiger, D. C., and Power, P. G. *My Vocational Situation.* Palo Alto, Calif.: Consulting Psychologists Press, 1980.

Johnston, J. A., and Hansen, R. N. "Using Paraprofessionals in Career Development Programming." In L. Harren, M. H. Daniels, and J. N. Buck (eds.), *Facilitating Students' Career Development.* San Francisco: Jossey-Bass, 1981.

Jung, C. G. *Memories, Dreams, Reflections.* (A. Jaffe, ed.; R. Winston and C. Winston, trans.) New York: Pantheon Books, 1961.

Krumboltz, J. D. *The Career Beliefs Inventory.* Palo Alto, Calif.: Consulting Psychologists Press, 1991.

Kurfiss, J. G. *Critical Thinking: Theory, Research, Practice, and Possibilities.* ASHE-ERIC Higher Education Reports, no. 2. Washington, D.C.: Association for the Study of Higher Education, 1988.

Larson, L., Heppner, P. P., Ham, T., and Dugan, K. "Investigating Multiple Subtypes of Career Indecision Through Cluster Analysis." *Journal of Counseling Psychology,* 1988, *35,* 349–446.

Levinson, D. J. *The Seasons of a Man's Life.* New York: Knopf, 1978.

Lopez, F. F., and Andrews, S. "Career Indecision: A Family Systems Perspective." *Journal of Counseling and Development,* 1987, *65,* 304–307.

McAuliffe, G. T. "Assessment and Treating Barriers to Decision Making in Career Classes." *Career Development Quarterly,* 1991, *40* (1), 82–92.

Neugarten, B. L. "Adult Personality: A Developmental View." *Human Development,* 1966, *9,* 61–73.

Parham, T. A., and Helms, J. E. "The Influence of Black Students' Racial Identity Attitudes on Preference for Counselor's Race." *Journal of Counseling Psychology,* 1981, *28,* 250–257.

Parsons, F. *Choosing a Vocation.* Boston: Houghton Mifflin, 1909.

Perry, W. G. *Forms of Intellectual and Ethical Development in the College Years: A Scheme.* Troy, Mo.: Holt, Rinehart & Winston, 1970.

Raimy, V. C. (ed.). *Training in Clinical Psychology (Boulder Conference).* New York: Prentice Hall, 1950.

Salomone, P. R. "Difficult Cases in Career Counseling, Part 2: The Indecisive Client." *Personnel and Guidance Journal,* 1982, *60,* 496–500.

Sanford, N. *Self and Society.* New York: Atherton, 1966.

Sheehy, G. *Passages: Predictable Crises of Adult Life.* New York: Dutton, 1974.

Smith, E. J. "Issues in Racial Minorities' Career Behavior." In W. B. Walsh and S. H. Osipow (eds.), *Handbook of Vocational Psychology.* Vol. 1. Hillsdale, N.J.: Erlbaum, 1983.

Snyder, C. R., Harris, C., Anderson, J. A., Irving, L. M., Sigmon, S. T., Yoshinobu, L., Gibb, J., Langelle, C., and Harney, P. "The Will and the Ways: Development and Validation of an Individual-Difference Measure of Hope." *Journal of Personality and Social Psychology,* 1991, *60,* 570–585.

Sue, D. W., and Sue, D. *Counseling the Culturally Different.* (2nd ed.) New York: Wiley, 1991.

Super, D. E. "A Life-Span, Life-Space Approach to Career Development." *Journal of Vocational Behavior,* 1980, *16,* 282–298.

Vaillant, G. E. "Theoretical Hierarchy of Adaptive Ego Mechanisms." *Archives of General Psychiatry,* 1971, *24,* 107–118.

MARY J. HEPPNER *is assistant professor of psychology and counseling psychologist at the Career Planning and Placement Center, University of Missouri, Columbia.*

JOSEPH A. JOHNSTON *is director of the Career Planning and Placement Center and professor of educational and counseling psychology at the University of Missouri.*

*This chapter discusses issues from needs assessment and programming for the majority, to programming for special populations and topics, to program evaluation. It also touches on experiential learning programs. Included are over one hundred programming ideas from the author's 1992 national survey of career center directors and an appendix of contact information on their programs.*

# Career Programming in a Contemporary Context

*Jean M. Yerian*

Along with placement services and career counseling services, career programming plays a vital role in today's comprehensive career services center. The Council for the Advancement of Standards for Student Services and Development Programs (CAS, 1986) identified three essential areas for a career planning and placement program: career counseling, placement counseling and referral, and student employment. But the variety of programming that colleges and universities have developed to address these areas goes far beyond any suggestions in the CAS standards and guidelines.

This chapter begins with an examination of the context for career programming and of various approaches to needs assessment, including focus groups. Typical "majority" programming is the next topic, with creative examples from career centers nationwide. The bulk of the chapter is about programming for special populations: persons with disabilities; racial and ethnic minorities; gay, lesbian, and bisexual students; returning adults (especially women); employees; alumni; and international students. There are brief references to experiential learning programs and other special programs, as well as to the evaluation of programs. Over one hundred ideas for programming from colleges and universities around the country are cited, and from them practitioners can gain both a sense of "what's out there" now and a stimulus for programming renewal on their own campuses (see the appendix for contact information on these programs).

## Needs Assessment

The creation of viable programming depends on an understanding of and adequate response to the unique needs of those served by the career center.

Belcher and Warmbrod (1987) stated that comprehensive, well-planned programs address both goals and objectives based on the needs of those served and the activities that can help participants achieve those desired outcomes.

**Evaluating the Context for Programming.** One approach to educational evaluation is the context-input-process-produce model (Stufflebeam and Shinkfield, 1985), which names four aspects of evaluation geared toward program improvement. If career centers fail to adequately evaluate the context in which career programming and other services are offered, "standard" programs may remain unexamined for years, like the proverbial yellowed notes of a tenured professor.

Meanwhile, college and university populations are changing dramatically. To keep current, there are many questions that a career center should ask: Who are the students, employers, alumni, and others who seek help? Who is present on the campus but absent from the career center? Which majors or special populations see themselves in career center offerings and which are invisible? Which academic departments do such an excellent job of working with their majors on career issues that little else is needed from the career center, and which departments tend to decry their students' preoccupation with "vocationalism," leaving their majors adrift and in need of special assistance?

Bhaerman (1985) offers more than a hundred "questions for action planning." While the goal of his questions is to inspire planning for adult career counseling, most of the questions apply to any form of career program planning. In the executive summary of his report, a simple statement appears: "Practitioners and policymakers need information about the populations whom they serve" (Bhaerman, 1985, p. vii).

**Determining Student Needs.** There are many viable ways to approach the needs assessment issue. Dickinson School of Law in Carlisle, Pennsylvania, does an annual survey of enrolled students. The University of Illinois uses a variety of methods: questionnaires to graduating students, attendance at monthly meetings of student organization leaders, a student advisory group, and feedback from graduate assistants and student workers in the office. The University of Tampa has students evaluate staff and services and also receives feedback from its Career Planning Model Committee. York College of Pennsylvania uses an "action research model," constantly evaluating, listening to student feedback, and implementing program ideas.

Other successful approaches include random telephone surveys, meetings with majors from individual departments of schools, tracking of program participation patterns and departmental enrollment shifts, discussions with faculty and student government representatives, and surveys conducted during academic registration periods. At Virginia Commonwealth University, a coordinating council made up of career center, cooperative education, counseling, advising, academic support, and academic unit representatives examines career support issues for which no one office has responsibility and sets its own agenda and action goals to address student needs that might otherwise fall through the cracks.

**Using Focus Groups.** Many in career services know the pioneering work of Cannon (1991) in relation to "Generation X" issues, based on focus group research with students in Canada, the United States, and the United Kingdom. The University of Pittsburgh did a focus group with undergraduates, seniors, and alumni to discover their needs and wants and to formulate approaches to better serving career center clients. Service users responded to a series of questions, proposing services they felt might be valuable to freshmen, sophomores, juniors, seniors, and, finally, alumni. Robert R. Perkoski, the University of Pittsburgh's director of career services, characterized the student focus groups as helping to "establish a dialogue . . . so that we don't simply assume that we know what's best for them" (personal communication, July 27, 1992). Regardless of the needs assessment approach used, career center staff must seriously and actively challenge their assumptions.

## Programming for the Majority

Virtually every career center has programs that teach participants the basics of career planning and job seeking. Usually, these programs assist students in assessing career interests and values, exploring educational and occupational options, making decisions regarding employment or graduate study, and building skills in résumé writing, interviewing, and job seeking. The center may also offer mock interviewing, help with choosing a major, and sponsor career fairs designed for the entire campus community.

Programs may expand students' understanding of computerized career systems such as DISCOVER, SIGI PLUS, and OPTIONS. The widespread adoption of such computerized career systems has given career centers valuable adjuncts to individual and group counseling, allowing students to benefit from the impressive data storage and retrieval capabilities of the Information Age. The structure of the systems parallels the career development theories most often embraced by career counselors; the occupational data within the systems clearly surpass in volume and currency what even the best centers can maintain without the use of computers. Most research reinforces the notion, though, that counselor contact complements the computer's strengths; the "high-tech, high-touch" approach seems the best combination.

The types of programs just described appear in most career centers and are designed to address common elements across student subpopulations. Such programs, properly done, form a valuable core. They are not, however, necessarily sufficient, and many career centers have a greater scope of general programming. At Bluefield State College in West Virginia, there is the Career

Counseling, Academic Advising, and Placement Center, where self-assess-ment inventories and campus interviewing are offered side-by-side with programs ranging from note taking to self-defense, to life management. At Norwich University in Northfield, Vermont, the popular "Tuesdays at Noon" series features relaxed, informal discussions of job research topics over a box lunch. At the University of Illinois in Urbana-Champaign, there are "Thurs-days at 4," designed to take advantage of the least-used class time and the most heavily used facility (the undergraduate library). At the University of the South in Sewanee, Tennessee, the "Looking Ahead" series generates a career portfolio, with résumé and sample cover letter, as well as self-assessment exercises.

The University of Alabama offers an in-house résumé service, producing thousands of custom résumés and cover letters each year. At Winthrop University in Rock Hill, South Carolina, there are separate program empha-ses and marketing strategies for freshmen through seniors. Rivier College in Nashua, New Hampshire, combats limited staffing with "self-made" video-tapes designed to introduce the career planning process and to follow up on use of computer-assisted guidance (Posluszny, 1992). Some colleges show videotaped programs on campus television channels transmitted to the residence halls and also make such tapes available to students for overnight and weekend checkout.

The idea is to recognize what will work on a given campus and then stretch programming resources—staff and funding alike—to the maximum. Two excellent sources of programming ideas are the Spotlight features of the *Career Waves* newsletter and the annual special awards reports of the *Journal of Career Planning and Employment* (usually in the fall issues).

Collaborative efforts are also important. Casella (1990) has argued for a new career center paradigm, contending that career centers have been evolving in purpose from job placement (1940s and 1950s) to career planning (1960s, 1970s, and 1980s), to career networking (1990s and beyond), with "connectedness" as the new central rationale. The National Career Development Association Professional Standards Committee (1992, p. 383) included in its career counseling competence statement both "ability to establish and maintain a productive consultation relationship with people in roles who can influence the client's career" and "knowledge of community/professional resources to assist clients in career/life planning, including job search." Casella (1990) talked about the shift in activities location from job interview rooms to offices and workshops, to on- and off-campus sites. These messages seem to be sinking in, in programming as well as in individual career services. It is no longer enough to sit back or be solitary.

Arizona State University staff go into classrooms and cosponsor pro-gramming series with two of the university's colleges. Ohio State University staff are currently planning a four-credit career and basic business skills development course to be required of all undergraduates in business. George Washington University's Career Week represents the collective efforts of alumni, faculty, and students, featuring more than sixty-five career information programs and three hundred presenters and drawing over twenty-six hundred people annually. Saint John's College in Annapolis, Maryland, has "Career Talk" conversations with professionals from different fields; Saint Mary's University School of Law in San Antonio, Texas, is instituting a "Day in the Life of . . ." series, with speakers who address different career areas. The University of the Arts in Philadelphia sponsors Career Day for Seniors, offering portfolio reviews and roundtable discussions with alumni and others; topics range from understanding potential career paths and getting into a gallery to keeping financial records and working with an artists' representative. In each of these cases, the programming fits the student community; in each, it goes beyond business as usual. And size has little to do with innovation.

Ideas abound. Saint Norbert College in De Pere, Wisconsin, sponsors "Networks," afternoon events in Chicago, the Fox Cities, Milwaukee, and the Twin Cities, with each student in attendance doing four informational interviews at a central site with representatives from the work world; the programs occur during school breaks. The School of Law at the State University of New York in Buffalo brings in attorneys from the Buffalo area to conduct practice interview workshops, where small groups of students participate in interviews of less than ten minutes, hearing feedback from the interviewer and from other students.

Wellesley College combines a luncheon panel presentation and after-lunch networking with the alumnae present at the event; each event has a theme, such as careers in communications. Wellesley also sponsors one-day chances for students to "shadow" alumnae during the January intersession, covering a dozen cities in the United States and a few sites abroad. Increasing numbers of schools have alumni who volunteer to help students with career information. The Stephens College Alumnae Career Consultants File, for example, has over two thousand volunteers from a variety of career fields; their computerized information is available by career field and geographical location.

General programming such as the examples given here can conserve and expand staff resources while achieving greater visibility and recognition. Each career center should consider what "return" it gets on the various "investments" that staff make. There is much evidence to suggest that the paradigm shift is real, that the magnet activity of campus recruiting is actually in decline. Rather than lament that trend, centers must develop other programs to compete with recruitment as the core activities.

## Programming for Special Populations

Many times the most innovative programming a center does is for the special populations on campus, perhaps because there is little history or tradition to overturn or because staff must stop to consider real (as opposed to assumed) needs. Whatever the explanation, these programs may be the best bridge from the old to the new paradigm. For that reason alone, they are worth examining in some detail here.

**Persons with Disabilities.** One career center pursues and wins a grant to subsidize summer employment for students with disabilities, thus combating the lack-of-experience obstacle that they might otherwise face. Another center asks employers to provide company information in braille. A third works closely with the Vocational Rehabilitation Services Office on campus. Yet another develops a notebook for faculty to use in working with these students.

In career centers across the country, staff are struggling to examine current practices and understand the nuances of the Americans with Disabilities Act of 1992. Simpkins and Kaplan (1991, p. 45) have suggested that each career center "actively inform disabled students of its services, rather than merely accommodate the disabled students who happen by." Rabby and Croft (1991, pp. 50–51) have urged career center staff to follow six guidelines in working with persons with disabilities: "Think mainstream . . . avoid generic labeling . . . diversify your thinking . . . stimulate options but don't take charge . . . never simulate a disability . . . [regard] disability [as] not necessarily a handicap." The message? In this arena, assumptions simply will not work.

As career centers try to look at their programming through largely unfamiliar eyes, they should recall the necessity of doing adequate needs assessment. The University of Northern Iowa, for example, plans to convene a focus group from a student organization called Restrict Us Not. (Colleges considering discussions with similar target groups might use a stimulus such as the videotape *Profiling Careers of Disabled College Graduates* [Western College Placement Association and California State University, Long Beach, 1982].)

To inform students with disabilities about career services, staff may need to employ a number of approaches. Michigan State University has its service brochure on audiotape. The University of Wisconsin in Stout has a handout describing specialized services and resources, including an enlarged-print vacancy list. Communication requires creativity. Programming often involves collaboration as well.

At Towson State University in Maryland a special program targets students with disabilities as candidates for on-campus, part-time jobs; the program is a cooperative project coordinated by the career center and involving five other campus offices. Arizona State University has a model program in the areas of cultural diversity and affirmative action. Student Opportunity for Leadership through Internship Development is a two-semester course that joins students from diverse ethnic minority groups and students with disabilities in one program to learn the skills needed to empower themselves and to reach for their career aspirations. Faculty for the program are from the community, from student affairs, and from IBM (a loaned faculty person).

The use of outside resources again brings the career networking paradigm shift to mind. Staff can refer persons with disabilities to the IBM National Support Center for Persons with Disabilities in Atlanta (Honeck, 1991) to get information on adaptive devices for the workplace. Illinois students can participate in the Annual Disability Employment and Resource Conference for college students, sponsored by the Illinois Division of Rehabilitation Services, the University of Illinois Division of Rehabilitation Education, Illinois State University, and private sector employers. At Stanford University, students have access to the Stanford University Career Counseling and Experience for Stanford Students with Disabilities (SUCCESS). Through SUCCESS, students with disabilities gain "direct access to career-experience opportunities—including informational interviews, internships, and mentor relationships—with sixty employers that have expressed a real interest" (McCarty, 1990, p. 64). The key to each of these successful programs is the same sort of collaborative creativity that could enliven any programming done by the career center.

**Racial and Ethnic Minorities.** In a world trying to move from awareness to appreciation of differences, even the term *minorities* is controversial. Career center staff recognize that people of color are not in the minority in the world as a whole, and virtually every career services professional has some idea of the changes and challenges outlined in the *Workforce 2000 Executive Summary* (U.S. Department of Labor, 1987): according to Hudson Institute projections, "Non-whites, women, and immigrants will make up more than five-sixths of the net additions to the workforce between now and the year 2000." It is no surprise, then, that many career centers are focusing increased attention on minority group programs.

Such programs have a tremendous range, from a single workshop or print resource to corporate-funded employment at both bachelor's and master's levels. Career center collaboration with multicultural student groups or special support offices is similarly diverse, from the forwarding of minority scholarship information to cosponsorship of career weekends, job fairs, and formal networking.

Often the start of successful programming, whether for minority or majority students, is outreach. The University of California at San Diego telephones sophomore, junior, and senior minority students, inviting them to come to the career center (Murray, 1990). Case Western Reserve University in Cleveland tapped outside funding to create the student-run Careers Unlimited Corporation, through which minority students now formulate, promote, and participate in career workshops (Barnard, Burney, and Hurley, 1990). Some career centers support outreach efforts beyond their own campus populations. Stevens Institute of Technology in Hoboken, New Jersey, sponsors the Stevens Technical Enrichment Program, which addresses populations from seventh grade through graduate study. Once again, staff need to consider "return on investment," both short term and long term, when considering what level of effort to devote to which compelling idea.

Mentoring programs are very popular. At Charleston Southern University, target populations now include African American, women, and business administration students, with a new population added each semester. Mentors come from professional associations primarily, but also from civic clubs, churches, and other groups working with the university. The Association of American Colleges (1985, p. 12), reviewing results from over sixty colleges and universities in its Minority Achievement Program, drew this conclusion: "Contact with successful minority professionals can sustain students through difficult periods. Because some minority students have not known any black professionals personally, such contact can dispel career misconceptions." People support what they help build; nurturing a mentoring program in one area can mean gaining allies for nurturing in other areas.

The minority career fair is another popular program. The University of Texas at Austin has "tri-ethnic" fairs, involving African American, Hispanic, and Asian students. The University of Virginia invites students from all of the state's colleges and universities to attend its Minority Student Career Day, subsidizing bus transportation costs for other institutions from employer fees. The Indiana University Placement Offices plan the Developing Diversity for Work Force 2000 Multicultural Job Fair for candidates throughout the nation. And special career fairs are not necessarily negatives for nontarget populations; employer contacts made for one population can, with adequate follow-up, pay off for all students. The problem is to ensure that everyone understands that potential value.

Virginia Polytechnic Institute and State University does a series of programs in conjunction with the Black Cultural Center, with employers sharing in both funding and presentations. The University of Florida has cultural diversity programming created by a student advisory committee. The importance of such efforts becomes clear from the investment of external groups with a minority focus. The Hispanic Association of Colleges and Universities (HACU, 1991) included the following in a public policy agenda statement: "In the 1990s, HACU will . . . implement career development programs that promote the public sector hiring of Hispanic students, for example, . . . cooperative education programs, . . . summer internship programs, . . . [and] career fairs." The Council on Career Development for Minorities, once part of the College Placement Council, has a track record of special programming support for various minority groups nationwide.

Seton Hall University in South Orange, New Jersey, receives corporate funding to employ a minority student career development assistant. At Pennsylvania State University, a minority internship program provides undergraduate students at the University Park campus with experiences—sometimes for credit or pay, other times as volunteers—in settings related to their education and career goals. As part of the career center's minority student employment program, second-year minority law students at the University of Pittsburgh School of Law work as part-time clerks with Pittsburgh law firms.

Rutgers University has an African American, Hispanic, Asian, and Native American (AHANA) program that includes a speakers series (one or two panel discussions each semester), a career day (with seventy to eighty employers), two newsletters sent to all AHANA students, and a workshop on finding summer internships.

The University of North Carolina put together a program called Competitive Edge. That program focused on eight projects with minorities: a freshman survey, a black alumni survey, a session during black alumni homecoming, the Computerized Carolina Connection alumni information network, an externship program, a sophomore career planning orientation, the all-day Capstone Career Seminar, and a survival skills workshop to help seniors make the transition from campus to workplace. The final verdict? "Comprehensive, high-visibility, and targeted programming are the keys to serving the career counseling needs of minority students" (Jones, 1992, p. 40).

Finally, career centers may address majority sensitivity to diversity issues. Temple University presented a workshop titled "The Dynamics of Working in a Multicultural Work Place." As part of Black History Month, the University of Wisconsin at Parkside held a program to help *all* students understand equal employment opportunity and affirmative action issues. Given the current makeup of the U.S. supervisory work force, such programming for the majority seems an excellent, responsible investment.

**Gay, Lesbian, and Bisexual Students.** There is no doubt that stereotypes of this population abound and that the stereotyping extends beyond sexual preference to occupational preference as well. But as Stewart (1991, p. 43) has observed, the stereotypes are seriously flawed: "According to a survey of 4,000 gay men and lesbians conducted by Overlooked Opinions, a Chicago market research firm, more homosexuals work in science and engineering than in social services; 40 percent more are employed in finance and insurance than in entertainment and the arts; and ten times as many work in computers as in fashion." According to Stewart, the current agenda for gay advocates includes "making discrimination according to sexual orientation as impermissible as discrimination according to race, age, or gender; promoting 'diversity training' to encourage work place tolerance; and lobbying for benefits that heterosexuals enjoy, mainly health insurance for partners" (p. 43). But these are issues largely missing from college career center programming. In fact, gay, lesbian, and bisexual (GLB) students probably experience less programming directed to their special needs than do any of the other populations listed here.

Still, survey data reveal some attempts to rectify this deficit. At several schools, there are staff members assigned as liaisons to the GLB student organizations that serve as the focal points for targeted programs on campus. Philip Martin, director of GLB student services for Ohio State University, recommends that all career center staff become more familiar with GLB issues by reading gay newspapers and basic books such as Blumenfeld and Raymond's (1988) *Looking at Gay and Lesbian Life* to gain a sense of both life-style and legal issues. Kathy Obear of the Human Advantage in Amherst, Massachusetts, recommends that her career center clients develop tools such as stimulus vignettes on illegal questions and remember to weave diversity concerns through all workshops and handouts.

A few career centers are already pursuing more extensive efforts. At the University of Pennsylvania, a flyer shows a modified Men at Work highway sign, announcing a "Gay Men and Lesbians at Work" speaker series co-sponsored with a GLB student group and featuring a session on opportunities and rights in the workplace, a panel of lesbian and gay employees, and a report from professional caucuses and search consultants titled "How We're Doing." Simmons College in Boston disseminates information on Lotus Corporation's family benefits for gay and lesbian partners, on the Greater Boston Business Council (composed of gay and lesbian professionals and business owners), and on using the *Gayellow Pages: The National Edition* (1991) as a resource for jobs or internships serving the gay and lesbian community; the center also sponsors brown-bag lunches on career topics as part of the Gay and Lesbian Awareness week on campus.

Staff at the State University of New York at Binghamton recently wrote organizations to solicit career resource materials for a binder of materials on gay men, lesbians, bisexuals, and work. Related activities included enhancing relationships with the Gay People's Union and displaying pink "Advocates for Awareness" triangles in career center display cases around campus. Career center staff member Robert Hradsky (1992) developed a "diversity report card" to help colleges and universities answer the question "Is your career center gay friendly?" The topics for grading include resources, referral lists, staff awareness and comfort levels, student organization contacts, and policies. Any career center could benefit from the discussions surrounding this type of assessment.

**Returning Adults (Especially Women).** Whether the program is called Second Wind or Life Long Learning or the College of Weekend Studies, returning adults often receive special attention. Career center staff may work with the campus adult student organization, women's center, or reentry center. Bluefield State College has its Thirty Something Support Group. Other college and university career centers encourage family activities, give Saturday tours, extend hours of operation, support special brown-bag lunches, and even organize career weeks specifically designed for nontraditional students.

For community colleges and many urban universities, adult students actually constitute the majority. Curtin and Hecklinger (1981) developed the Career Life Assessment Skills Series, covering job keeping and revitalization and preretirement planning, as well as the more usual career topics. Haskell and Wiener (1986) urged attention in community colleges to such programming as job clubs, opportunity seminars for entering nontraditional fields, and dress-for-success workshops. Keierleber and Sundal-Hansen (1986, p. 260) have suggested that universities encourage "self-managed, ongoing support groups . . . around common issues or target populations such as veterans, reentry women, single parents, displaced workers, or men changing careers."

Adult programming is not just for currently enrolled students. The University of Portland has the Capstone Program for People in Transition, a cooperative venture of the adult programs office and the career center wherein community adults examine assets and options and then develop a personal plan, targeted at either returning to school or seeking an immediate job. New Mexico State University at Carlsbad has the Higher Education and Life Planning Center. Roger Williams University in Bristol, Rhode Island, sponsors a series of seminars, many with outside speakers. The career directions series is for women who are ready to explore options outside the home; they may subscribe to individual sessions or to the whole series. Such programming can serve to tie career centers into institutional recruitment or community service goals.

**Employees.** Ohio State University probably has the most unusual arrangement, a separate, full-service career center for faculty and staff. Few other centers have any mission or funding to serve the employees of their institutions. It is fairly common, however, for staff to provide individual assistance on request, at least at some minimal level.

Some career centers' staff also use their expertise to assist the institutions' faculty and staff with diversity issues, Myers-Briggs training, and other topics. Bowdoin College in Brunswick, Maine, conducts a training workshop for administrative managers on effective, lawful interviewing practices. Simmons College helps employees learn how to better interview and supervise student assistants. The University of Nevada at Reno holds special brown-bag career development lunches. At Temple University, there is a different emphasis. The career center does a job search workshop each December and July for all employees' sons and daughters who are graduating from college. The University of Pennsylvania has a similar program for faculty children. Jacksonville University makes all services and workshops available to employees, their spouses, and their teenage-or-older children.

All of these programs can stimulate positive perceptions of the career center and result in increased confidence and referrals of students. But they can also drain resources unnecessarily if the career center fails to clearly define boundaries and priorities.

**Alumni.** The same gain-or-drain argument can apply to services for the institution's own graduates, although alumni services are typically part of the career center's mission. Many staff refer alumni résumés, publish jobs in an alumni bulletin, coordinate workshops such as career alternatives for teachers, and conduct career changer groups on a regular basis. Some colleges and universities sponsor job fairs at the time of homecoming or have human resources alumni coach other graduates.

Sometimes the programming is a cooperative venture with the alumni activities office. At Pennsylvania State University, this takes the form of four day-long workshops a year, offered in four different locations. The University of Pittsburgh offers AlumNet, a data base designed to help alumni job seekers tap information from alumni who are already employed. Also in the electronic realm are commercial candidate data bases aimed at alumni; Duke University participates in one such program, called SkillSearch. At the University of Illinois, there is an entire center, which is actually a unit of the alumni association, that provides a variety of career services.

Simon Fraser University in British Columbia has several noteworthy cooperative ventures. One example is the free Alumni Job Finding Club, which targets those who have graduated within the prior two years and are available to job search full-time. The service provides telephones, typewriters, a photocopier, clerical support, stationery, handbooks, newspapers, and other support materials, with the goal of getting the recent graduate started on a degree-related career path. The results? "Success was beyond the wildest, optimistic imaginings—placement rates over 80 to 90 percent, respectively, for those who took part in the original sessions" (Mason, 1991, p. 5). The program now serves about twenty alumni each month.

Service approaches vary, as do funding sources. The Norwich University Career Network links successful alumni and alumni job seekers in eighteen occupations and industries across six geographical regions of the country. Elmhurst College in Illinois has an alumni support group program each month that highlights an industry or occupation and includes related interviewing tips from a human resources professional. The University of Alabama's alumni assistance program entails a fee for a package of services over a set subscription period. San Diego State University uses a "pay-as-you-go" approach, with several different fee-for-service options.

Just as staff invest time in alumni services, alumni invest time with students; several examples of such contributions appear elsewhere in this chapter. At Seton Hall University, there is a four-part series in which students define career goals, prepare for informational interviews, do those interviews with alumni, and then discuss the results in groups. At Washington and Lee University, alumni assist with recruitment, give career advice in person and by telephone, offer experiential learning opportunities, and help students adjust to new communities. As Heatley (1991, p. 51) has noted, "We were eager to have the alumni involvement because we knew they could produce tangible results." It is exactly such productivity that makes alumni services one of the best investments for a career center. Whether or not individual counseling accompanies programming and other services is a more difficult resource issue.

**International Students.** Most career center programming for international students tries to help them develop the skills to find permanent employment in their home countries and experiential learning opportunities in the United States. Virginia Polytechnic Institute and State University does programming on practical training, work eligibility, and immigration issues. Programs at the University of Texas at Austin include "Getting into Graduate School" and "Going Back to Your Home Country." Because of changing visa restrictions, career center staff seldom feel at ease giving specific directions on legal issues. Consequently, much programming occurs in cooperation with the international student advisers on campus.

There are also proactive programs, such as special résumé books, in which career center staff serve as advocates for international students. The University of Rochester career center has a course that allows international students to pursue summer internships. Jacksonville University arranges introductions to company representatives of international businesses; Michigan State University maintains an international employer network and sponsors a specialized career fair. There are also career fairs for international students at American University and throughout the Midwest, the latter targeted at M.B.A. students in Big Ten schools. At the University of Illinois in Urbana-Champaign, a program called ASEAN LINKAGES seeks to expand opportunities for Singaporean, Malaysian, Indonesian, Philippine, and Pacific Islander students through special orientations, information distribution, workshops, alumni contacts, a job fair trip, and a planned internship program.

Although there is much concern about the U.S. trade deficit, there is little doubt that American higher education is still a sought-after commodity. What career centers somehow must come to terms with is the development of specialized programming for international students that neither ignores their unique assets nor overpromises specific outcomes in terms of employment. To date, experiential learning programs seem to offer the most promise in striking this balance.

## Experiential Learning Programs

It is beyond the scope of this chapter to give anything like a complete picture of the experiential learning programs blossoming across the country today. Suffice it to say that many employers increasingly regard cooperative education, internships, externships, student employment programs, and even volunteer services as highly productive sources for college hires. The trend is dramatic, almost in direct contrast to the diminution of campus interviews.

At Clemson University in South Carolina, internship information is on the mainframe computer, accessible to all students. Students interested in internships register on a data base, which is sent to employers without charge. Connecticut College sponsors the month-long January Career Internship Program, with alumni coordinators in four East Coast areas. At Cornell University, the School of Industrial and Labor Relations sponsors the Winter Intersession Program, designed to introduce students to employers and establish relationships that could develop into summer jobs, semester internships, and even full-time employment following graduation. Elmhurst College uses a grant from the Illinois Cooperative Work Study Program for JOBPATH, a program to target organizations that have no prior experience with interns and to encourage employers with successful experiences to expand their participation. Harvard University focuses on spring break internships, while the University of Minnesota boasts the highly successful Professional Learning Experience Program for biology students. The University of Wisconsin at La Crosse has an exceptional international internship program.

The College of William and Mary in Williamsburg, Virginia, promotes internships, shared experiences, international work and study, community service, and campus activities in a single brochure, encouraging students to serve societal needs while gaining valuable experience. Duke University offers the semester-long Career Apprenticeship Program, as well as a health careers internship program and a service learning project. The University of Wisconsin at Parkside volunteer program's theme is "Making a Difference."

At Indiana University–Purdue University at Indianapolis, the Professional Practice Program has internship and cooperative education options, while Joint Opportunities for Business and Students attempts to identify employment that does not conflict with students' classes. The University of Virginia claims the largest externship program in the country, with over one thousand students a year participating in one-week, nonpaid experiences. Successful programs come in all shapes and sizes and even claim positive results for such special populations as students with disabilities.

There seems to be some trend toward consolidation of career services and experiential learning programs as budget and staff reductions continue in higher education; career centers should prepare to examine how these functions can best be supported. The College Placement Council offers informational packages on experiential education programs. In addition to over twenty articles, the packages include contact information for five experiential education organizations at the national level.

The list of special populations and topics is nearly endless, as is the potential for developing targeted programming. The University of Illinois at Urbana-Champaign boasts the Biotechnology Center Placement Office, where companies can seek advanced degree candidates and postdoctorate scholars for positions in biologically related areas. Harvard Law School expands student knowledge of public interest career options with a published guide (DeBroff, 1991), including eight pages on programs and services ranging from campus interviews and job fairs to fellowships, a toll-free telephone line, and summer work options. The University of Northern Iowa helps general studies majors learn how to plan their careers and tie their majors to the job market. Wellesley College offers a three-week survey of management basics for liberal arts students. American University staff assist with awards and fellowships for undergraduates and focus increased energies on graduate students, who are increasingly coming directly from baccalaureate programs, with little or no work experience. Stephens College endeavors to give students a feel for graduate study by inviting in alumnae and friends several times a year to share their graduate and professional school experiences.

Washington and Lee University has had good results from fraternity and sorority outreach programs. University of Nevada at Reno staff work with student athletes. George Washington University targets freshman liberal arts students in a number of ways, including a required orientation and advising course. Winthrop University's Get a Life party for freshmen acquaints them with career center services and establishes early use of resources. Roger Williams University has a workshop titled "How to Return Home and Negotiate with Parents." Boston College sponsors a weekend job search workshop for parents of seniors, followed by tours of the career center.

The State University of New York at Binghamton responded to tough economic times with a series of initiatives. Staff reached out to faculty, produced a special newsletter, answered questions on a radio call-in show, sent out "job alert" notices, contacted employers at a trade show held on campus, started a job search group, and created binders titled "One-Year Opportunities for After Graduation." Their proactive approach resulted in high student use of the center and positive interactions with others on campus.

At the Ringling School of Art and Design in Sarasota, Florida, the career center offers an amazing variety of programs for the artists that compose the school's student community. There are portfolio receptions, artist survival skills workshops and courses, a job bank hotline, internships, an alumni resource network, a shadow program over spring break, and even a full professional conference titled "The Next Step" for those graduating. The center addresses virtually every possible career issue for artists.

To strengthen services to the campus community and to employers, Clemson University requests nominations for juniors to be ambassadors of the Student Team Assisting with Recruiting Services. Students chosen act as liaisons between the career center and their respective academic areas, help at career fairs, coordinate visits with recruiters, and convey important announcements and events to other students. They also provide suggestions for career center planning. As stated earlier, successful programming often involves active outreach.

## Evaluation of Programs

Just as this review began with needs assessment, it ends with another form of assessment, the evaluation of products, outcomes, and results. Probably the most popular product evaluation of career centers is the annual follow-up survey of recent graduates to determine their employment and graduate study patterns. Often the survey becomes a document that is widely circulated and valued by the institution (especially if it shows that all is going according to plan). The other nearly ubiquitous publication is the annual report of the career center, detailing accomplishments and activities. And virtually every career center is part of the evaluation focus during periodic accreditation self-studies and visits. But these evaluations, while important, tend to be summative rather than formative, that is, they focus on what has been rather than what should be.

Some career centers do more extensive internal evaluations. West Chester University in Pennsylvania collects a use-and-satisfaction survey at commencement practice. An increasing number of career centers are using the CAS (1988) approach to self-study and program improvement. To get additional constructive criticism and challenge, career centers may turn to external reviews. At Charleston Southern University, the institutional research office does an overall evaluation for the center. Elsewhere, the outside reviewers come from one of the seven regional placement associations nationwide. Recently, the University of Wisconsin at Stout brought in an external consultant; some centers have such visits as five-year rotational program reviews.

Virginia Commonwealth University solicits written evaluations of virtually all programs and services, from individual and group career counseling, workshops, and classroom presentations to career fairs, campus interviews, student employment experiences, and office publications; such evaluations form the basis for a continuous improvement process linked to both staff and program development. Across the country, career centers are moving toward quality assessment as increasing numbers of their own institutions and the employers whom they serve examine and commit to Total Quality Management (TQM) principles and practices. Korschgen and Rounds (1992, p. 49) have highly recommended the application of such principles to career center services: "In the two years that we have focused on quality we have increased the number of students participating in our internship program from 337 to 361; reorganized our Career Day into a campus-wide event with 110 to 115 employers (instead of 65 in previous years) and 2,000 students attending (instead of 500); increased total student contacts by 2 percent; computerized the majority of our office functions; and eased our fiscal constraints so that we are beginning to upgrade office furniture and equipment." Not many staffs would knowingly turn down the chance for such positive changes, but few career centers have yet embraced TQM concepts. In an effort to encourage more extensive attention to evaluation, the College Placement Council recently formed the Measurement and Methodology Task Force.

The point should be clear: Individual career centers and professional associations alike must recognize the necessity of greater accountability and critically examine programs from conception to implementation, to evaluation, and back to reconceptualization. Career center staff know a similar progression from using career development cycle models with students; now it is time for them to apply context-input-process-produce or other evaluation models to their own work. The viability of career programming and perhaps even the survival of career centers are at stake. From a return-on-investment standpoint, evaluation is a low-cost, high-gain item.

## Conclusion

As should be apparent from the wealth of examples in this chapter, career centers are capable of great creativity in developing and implementing career programs that address the special needs of special people, whether majority students, students from diverse backgrounds, community members, or others. If staff are willing to do the tough up-front and follow-up work of assessment and evaluation, every center is capable of offering excellent and appropriate career programming.

## Appendix: Career Programming Models

American University, Career Center, 4400 Massachusetts Ave., N.W., Washington, DC 20016, (202) 885-1800.

Arizona State University, Career Services, Student Services Bldg., Rm. C359, Tempe, AZ 85287-1312, (602) 965-2350.

Bluefield State College, Placement, 219 Rock St., Bluefield, WV 24701, (304) 327-4011.

Boston College, Career Center, 38 Commonwealth Ave., Chestnut Hill, MA 02167, (617) 552-3435.

Bowdoin College, Career Services, Moulton Union, Brunswick, ME 04011, (207) 725-3717.

California State University at Long Beach, Career Development Center, 1250 Bellflower Blvd., Long Beach, CA 90840-0113, (310) 985-5554.

Case Western Reserve University, Career Planning and Placement Office, Pardee Hall, 10900 Euclid Ave., Cleveland, OH 44106-7040, (216) 368-4446.

Charleston Southern University, Career Planning and Placement, Box 10087, Charleston, SC 29411, (803) 863-8019.

Clemson University, Career Center, 804 University Student Union, Clemson, SC 29634-4007, (803) 656-2152.

College of William and Mary, Career Services, 123 Blow Memorial Hall, P. O. Box 8795, Williamsburg, VA 23187-8795, (804) 221-3240.

Connecticut College, Career Services, 270 Mohegan Ave., New London, CT 06320-4196, (203) 439-2770.

Cornell University, University Career Center, 103 Barnes Hall, Ithaca, NY 14853, (607) 255-5221.

Dickinson School of Law, Career Center, 150 S. College St., Carlisle, PA 17013-2848, (717) 240-5201.

Duke University, Career Development Center, Box 90950, Page Bldg., Durham, NC 27708-0950, (919) 660-1050.

Elmhurst College, Career Services, 190 Prospect, College Union Bldg., Elmhurst, IL 60126, (708) 617-3186.

George Washington University, Career and Cooperative Education Center, T-509 Academic Ctr., 801 22nd St., N.W., Washington, DC 20052, (202) 994-6495.

Harvard University, Career Services, 54 Dunster St., Cambridge, MA 02138, (617) 495-2595.

Harvard University School of Law, Public Interest Placement Advising Office, Cambridge, MA 02138, (617) 495-3108.

Indiana University, Career Development Center, 625 N. Jordan Ave., Bloomington, IN 47405, (812) 855-5234.

Indiana University–Purdue University at Indianapolis, Career and Employment Services, 801 W. Michigan St., Business/SPEA Bldg., Rm. 2010, Indianapolis, IN 46202-5153, (317) 274-2554.

Jacksonville University, Career Counseling and Placement, Howard Administration Bldg., Jacksonville, FL 32211, (904) 744-3950, ext. 2270.

Michigan State University, Career Development and Placement Services, 113 Student Services Bldg., East Lansing, MI 48824, (517) 355-9510.

New Mexico State University at Carlsbad, Higher Education and Life Planning Center, 1500 University Dr., Carlsbad, NM 88220, (505) 885-8831, ext. 223.

Norwich University, Career Development Center, Northfield, VT 05663, (802) 485-2125.

Ohio State University, College of Business, Career Development Services, 1775 College Rd., Columbus, OH 43210, (614) 292-6024.

Pennsylvania State University, University Park Campus, Career Development and Placement Services, 417 Boucke Bldg., University Park, PA 16802, (814) 865-2377.

Ringling School of Art and Design, Center for Career Services, 2700 N. Tamiami Trail, Sarasota, FL 34234, (813) 359-7500.

Rivier College, Career Development and Placement, 429 S. Main St., Nashua, NH 03060, (603) 888-1311, ext. 245.

Roger Williams University, Career Services, Ferry Rd., Maple Hall, Bristol, RI 02809, (401) 254-3540.

Rutgers University, New Brunswick Campus, Career Services, 542 George St., P. O. Box 5066, New Brunswick, NJ 08903-5066, (908) 932-7353.

Saint John's College, Placement, P. O. Box 2800, Annapolis, MD 21404, (301) 263-2371, ext. 200.

Saint Mary's University School of Law, Career Services, San Antonio, TX 78228-8517, (512) 436-3511.

Saint Norbert College, College Placement Services, 100 Grant St., De Pere, WI 54115-2099, (414) 337-3040.

San Diego State University, Career Services, Student Services Bldg., Rm. 1200, San Diego, CA 92182-0578, (619) 594-6851.

Seton Hall University, Career Services, Bayley Hall, South Orange, NJ 07079-2679, (201) 761-9355.

Simon Fraser University, Placement Centre, Room AQ 3044, Burnaby, BC, Canada V5A 1S6, (604) 291-3105.

Simmons College, Career Services and Student Employment Office, 300 The Fenway, Boston, MA 02115, (617) 738-2115.

Stanford University, Career Planning and Placement Center, White Memorial Plaza, Stanford, CA 94305, (415) 723-3963.

State University of New York at Binghamton, Career Development Center, P. O. Box 6013, Binghamton, NY 13902-6013, (607) 777-2191.

State University of New York at Buffalo School of Law, Career Development Office, 309 O'Brian Hall, Buffalo, NY 14260, (716) 636-2056.

Stephens College, Career Services, Box 2123, Columbia, MO 65215, (314) 876-7101.

Stevens Institute of Technology, Career Services, Castle Point Station, Hoboken, NJ 07030, (201) 216-5166.

Temple University, Career Development Center, Mitten Hall, Philadelphia, PA 19122, (215) 787-7981.

Towson State University, Career Placement Center, 217 University Union, Towson, MD 21204, (410) 830-2233.

University of Alabama, Placement Office, Tuscaloosa, AL 35487-0293, (205) 348-5848.

University of California at San Diego, Career Services Center, 9500 Gilman Dr., La Jolla, CA 92093-0330, (619) 534-3750.

University of Florida, Career Resource Center, G-1, Reitz Union, Gainesville, FL 32611-2042, (904) 392-1601.

University of Illinois, Alumni Career Center, 412 S. Peoria St., 4400 Alumni Hall, MC024, Chicago, IL 60607, (312) 996-6350.

University of Illinois, Biotechnology Center, 105 Observatory, 901 S. Mathews Ave., Urbana, IL 61801, (217) 333-1695.

University of Illinois, Career Services Center, 610 E. John St., Student Services Bldg., Rm. 310, Champaign, IL 61820, (217) 333-0820.

University of Minnesota, College of Biological Sciences, 1475 Gortner Ave., 217 Snyder Hall, Saint Paul, MN 55108, (612) 624-9270.

University of Nevada at Reno, Career Development/104, Reno, NV 89557, (702) 784-4678.

University of North Carolina, University Career Services, 211 Hanes Hall, Chapel Hill, NC 27514, (919) 962-6507.

University of Northern Iowa, Placement and Career Services, Student Services Center, No. 19, Cedar Falls, IA 50614-0384, (319) 273-2068.

University of Pennsylvania, University Career Planning and Placement Service, 3718 Locust Walk, McNeil Bldg., Ste. 20, Philadelphia, PA 19104, (215) 898-3208.

University of Pittsburgh, University Placement Service, 236 William Pitt Union, Pittsburgh, PA 15260, (412) 648-7130.

University of Pittsburgh School of Law, Placement Office, 3900 Forbes Ave., Pittsburgh, PA 15260, (412) 648-1411.

University of Portland, Career Services, 5000 N. Willamette Blvd., University Center for Counseling and Health, Portland, OR 97203, (503) 283-7201.

University of Rochester, Center for Work and Career Development, 224 Lattimore Hall, Rochester, NY 14627, (716) 275-2366.

University of the South, Career Services, 2 Cleveland Memorial, Sewanee, TN 37375, (615) 598-1121.

University of Tampa, Personnel and Career Development Center, 401 W. Kennedy Blvd., Tampa, FL 33606-1490, (813) 253-6218.

University of Texas at Austin, Career Center, Jester A115, Austin, TX 78705, (512) 471-1217.

University of the Arts, Placement Office, Broad and Pine Streets, Philadelphia, PA 19102, (215) 875-1069.

University of Virginia, Career Planning and Placement, Garrett Hall, Charlottesville, VA 22903, (804) 924-8900.

University of Wisconsin at La Crosse, Career Services, Wilder Hall, La Crosse, WI 54601, (608) 785-8514.

University of Wisconsin at Parkside, Career Center, 900 Wood Rd., Box 2000, Kenosha, WI 53141, (414) 595-2452.

University of Wisconsin at Stout, Career Services, Administration Bldg., Menomonie, WI 54751, (715) 232-1602.

Virginia Commonwealth University, University Career Center, 907 Floyd Ave., Box 2007, Richmond, VA 23284-2007, (804) 367-1645.

Virginia Polytechnic Institute and State University, University Placement Services, Henderson Hall, Blacksburg, VA 24061-0128, (703) 231-6241.

Washington and Lee University, Career Development and Placement, University Center, Lexington, VA 24450, (703) 463-8595.

Wellesley College, Career Center, Wellesley, MA 02181, (617) 283-2352.

West Chester University, Career Development Center, Lawrence Hall 106, West Chester, PA 19383, (215) 436-2501.

Winthrop University, Career Services, 638 W. Oakland Ave., Rock Hill, SC 29733, (803) 323-2141.

York College of Pennsylvania, Career Services Center, York, PA 17405-7199, (717) 846-7788, ext. 228.

*Source:* College Placement Council, 1993.

# References

Association of American Colleges. *Helping Minority Students Succeed.* Washington, D.C.: Association of American Colleges, 1985.

Barnard, C., Burney, D. A., and Hurley, J. "Involving Minority Students in Career Services." *Journal of Career Planning and Employment,* 1990, *50* (3), 43–47.

Belcher, J. O., and Warmbrod, C. P. *Adult Career Guidance.* Columbus: National Center for Research in Vocational Education, Ohio State University, 1987.

Bhaerman, R. D. *Planning for Adult Career Counseling.* Columbus: National Center for Research in Vocational Education, Ohio State University, 1985.

Blumenfeld, W. J., and Raymond, D. *Looking at Gay and Lesbian Life.* Boston: Beacon Press, 1988.

Cannon, D. "Generation X: The Way They Do the Things They Do." *Journal of Career Planning and Employment,* 1991, *51* (2), 34–38.

Casella, D. A. "Career Networking—the Newest Career Center Paradigm." *Journal of Career Planning and Employment,* 1990, *50* (4), 32–39.

College Placement Council. *College Placement Council Directory.* Bethlehem, Pa.: College Placement Council, 1993.

Council for the Advancement of Standards for Student Services and Development Programs (CAS). *CAS Standards and Guidelines for Student Services and Development Programs.* Washington, D.C.: CAS, 1986.

Council for the Advancement of Standards for Student Services and Development Programs (CAS). *Career Planning and Placement Self-Assessment Guide.* Washington, D.C.: CAS, 1988.

Curtin, B. M., and Hecklinger, F. J. *The Career Life Assessment Skills Series (CLASS).* Alexandria: Northern Virginia Community College, 1981.

DeBroff, S. M. *Public Interest Job Search Guide.* Cambridge, Mass.: Harvard Law School, Harvard University, 1991.

*Gayellow Pages: The National Edition.* New York: Renaissance House, 1991.

Haskell, P., and Wiener, N. "Career Counseling Adults in a Community College Setting." In Z. B. Leibowitz and H. D. Lea (eds.), *Adult Career Development: Concepts, Issues, and Practices.* Alexandria, Va.: American Association for Counseling and Development, 1986.

Heatley, R. "Alumni Career Assistance Program (for Students)." *Journal of Career Planning and Employment,* 1991, *52* (1), 51–52.

Hispanic Association of Colleges and Universities. *Public Policy Agenda for the 1990s.* San Antonio, Tex.: Hispanic Association of Colleges and Universities, 1991.

Honeck, J. "IBM's Focus: On Employees' Abilities . . . *Not* Their Disabilities." *Journal of Career Planning and Employment,* 1991, *51* (2), 68–71.

Hradsky, R. D. "Responding to Gay/Lesbian/Bisexual Student Needs." Paper presented at the State University of New York Career Development Organization Conference, Alexandria Bay, New York, 1992.

Jones, S. L. "Providing Minority Students with the Competitive Edge." *Journal of Career Planning and Employment,* 1992, *52* (3), 36–40.

Keierleber, D. L., and Sundal-Hansen, L. S. "Adult Career Development in University Settings: Practical Perspectives." In Z. B. Leibowitz and H. D. Lea (eds.), *Adult Career Development: Concepts, Issues, and Practices.* Alexandria, Va.: American Association for Counseling and Development, 1986.

Korschgen, A. J., and Rounds, D. "Quality Management in Career Services, à la Deming." *Journal of Career Planning and Employment,* 1992, *52* (4), 47–50.

McCarty, A. "SUCCESS—Stanford University Career Counseling and Experience for Stanford Students with Disabilities." *Journal of Career Planning and Employment,* 1990, *51* (1), 64.

Mason, B. "Alumni Learn a Living." *Simon Fraser Alumni Journal,* 1991, *9* (1), 5–6.

Murray, N. "How to Attract More Women and Minorities to the Career Center." *Journal of Career Planning and Employment,* 1990, *50* (2), 26.

National Career Development Association Professional Standards Committee. "Career Counseling Competencies." *Career Development Quarterly,* 1992, *40* (4), 378–386.

Posluszny, S. B. "Career-Counseling Them All—and on a Limited Budget." *Journal of Career Planning and Employment,* 1992, *52* (4), 51–53.
Rabby, R., and Croft, D. "Working with Disabled Students: Some Guidelines." *Journal of Career Planning and Employment,* 1991, *51* (2), 49–54.
Simpkins, K. L., and Kaplan, R. K. "Fair Play for Disabled Persons: Our Responsibilities Under the New ADA." *Journal of Career Planning and Employment,* 1991, *51* (2), 40–46.
Stewart, T. A. "Gay in Corporate America." *Fortune,* 1991, *124* (14), 42–56.
Stufflebeam, D. L., and Shinkfield, A. J. *Systematic Evaluation.* Boston: Kluwer-Nijhoff, 1985.
U.S. Department of Labor. *Workforce 2000 Executive Summary.* Washington, D.C.: Government Printing Office, 1987.
Western College Placement Association and California State University, Long Beach. *Profiling Careers of Disabled College Graduates.* 1982. Videotape.

JEAN M. YERIAN *is director of University Career Center at Virginia Commonwealth University, Richmond, Virginia, and serves as the College Placement Council's director on the Council for the Advancement of Standards for Student Services and Development Programs.*

*Themes common to all of the chapters in this volume are summarized,*
*and ten imperatives for career centers in the 1990s are presented.*

# Concluding Remarks and Career Services Imperatives for the 1990s

*Jack R. Rayman*

Each of the previous chapters focuses on issues that now confront and will continue to confront career services professionals in the 1990s. The authors provide their individual perspectives on different aspects of contemporary career services and generously share their experience and expertise. In this final chapter, I identify issue-oriented threads that are interwoven through all five chapters, and I attempt to fashion those common threads into a set of ten imperatives for the career services profession in the 1990s.

IMPERATIVE 1. *We must acknowledge the lifelong nature of career development and initiate programs and services that enable and encourage students to take responsibility for their own career destiny.*

In Chapter One, I attempted to underscore this point by presenting a career development paradigm that provides a theoretical rationale for the establishment and maintenance of comprehensive career services. All of this volume's authors acknowledge the reality of this imperative. If we accomplish nothing else in the 1990s, we must, by our actions, convey to students that they will need to be proactive in their pursuit of their personal career development. The passive approach to seeking employment is no longer appropriate or effective. The field of career services has entered a new era.

IMPERATIVE 2. *We must accept and embrace technology as our ally and shape its use to free staff time for those tasks that require human sensitivity.*

All of the functional areas within the career center are likely to be affected significantly by technological change. In Chapter Three, Stewart suggests that technology is likely to be the salvation for placement in the 1990s. The following are key aspects of career services operations that are likely to be positively affected by technology:

**Electronic Storage, Retrieval, and Transmission of Credentials.** Student and alumni credentials will be entered, stored, retrieved, and then transmitted to employers electronically. Improved scanning technology will allow the rapid entry of student data into electronic storage, eliminating costly and time-consuming data entry. Through such initiatives as the Data Sheet Interchange Standard, or DASIS, compatibility of hardware and software will be achieved, and an industry standard will be established that will allow thousands of résumés and other credentials to be exchanged among career centers and employers nationally and internationally. This technological revolution is likely to reduce significantly the clerical support that is necessary to operate a modern placement office and will lead to the establishment of national and internal credential banks. Such credential banks will facilitate the trend toward the globalization of business.

**Computer-Administered and -Interpreted Assessment.** Time limitations that often preclude the use of various assessment devices in career counseling will be overcome through the increased use of computer-delivered assessment devices. By the end of this decade, nearly all standardized tests and other assessment devices are likely to be delivered by computer. Many will also be interpreted by computer.

**Video Interviewing.** Video telephone interviewing is already being used to supplement on-campus interviewing on a limited basis (DeShong, Davis, Peterson, and Rayman, 1990). As the technology continues to improve and the costs decrease, video interviews will become a viable alternative to on-campus interviews. While such techniques are not likely to replace on-campus interviews in the 1990s, they almost certainly will have an impact.

**Computer-Assisted Career Guidance.** Computer-assisted career guidance and counseling will become ever more sophisticated, helpful, and pervasive (Rayman, 1990). This trend will enhance career center productivity by freeing counselor time for those tasks that require human sensitivity.

**Voice Mail.** As frustrating as we sometimes find voice mail, it is here to stay, and further refinements will ensure the continuation of its important role in enhancing the efficiency of the career center of the 1990s. Voice-mail job listing services are already beginning to take off, and other applications seem likely to follow.

**New and Forthcoming Technology.** As I have pointed out elsewhere, "One key to new developments will be new technology probably in the form of the compact laser disc. Such discs will support significant innovation in terms of high resolution graphics, full motion video and enhanced sound capabilities. The laser disc and other innovations will play a key role in the development of subsystems to meet the career development needs of the expanded populations that we now serve. The aural and visual dimensions that will become available through the utilization of new technology offer great promise for users with hearing, reading, and other deficiencies and/or disabilities" (Rayman, 1990, p. 258).

IMPERATIVE 3. *We must continue to refine and strengthen our professional identity and that of career services within the academy.*

In Chapter Two, Bechtel reflects the feelings of many career services professionals in expressing his concern about the ambiguity surrounding the role, mission, and organizational relationship of the modern career center within the academic community. Similarly, the future status of the profession remains ambiguous, with different professional associations vying to represent career services professionals. As Bechtel suggests, we need to clean up our act. We need to fight our way through the organizational morass and the professional ambiguity and emerge from this decade with a clearer professional identity and a stronger sense of mission and purpose. If we are to ensure our viability in the academic environment, we must develop the self-confidence to be our own strong advocates. To paraphrase Stewart, if we are to succeed, we must be our own advocates, and we must be able to articulate our place within the academy. It is my hope that the standards and guidelines of the Council for the Advancement of Standards for Student Services and Development Programs (1988) will be helpful to us in this regard.

IMPERATIVE 4. *We must acknowledge and accept that individual career counseling is at the core of our profession, and endeavor to maintain and enhance the centrality of individual career counseling in the career development process.*

Although the individual chapter authors deal with different functions and aspects of career services, each has acknowledged in one way or another the need to keep individual career counseling at the core of the career development process. While Heppner and Johnston, in Chapter Four, suggest innovative ways in which peer counselors can be used to supplement professional counseling, and Stewart looks to technology as a way to free professional staff time, implicit in their assumptions is an acknowledgment that individual career counseling is at the core of the career services enterprise, and that only through the implementation of innovative delivery systems, such as those described by Yerian in Chapter Five, and the effective use of technology can we free staff time for the important work of counseling.

While the placement function remains important, economic and social forces clearly dictate that the career development, career counseling, and career education functions take on even more importance in the 1990s. The challenge of meeting the increasingly diverse career development needs of an increasingly diverse student body will compel us to shift from the dominant point-in-time, one-service-fits-all placement model of the past to a lifelong process, differential diagnosis and differential treatment model of the future, where individual counseling will be central.

Finally, in the impersonal world of large universities where classes of five hundred or more students are the norm, where televised lectures abound, and advising is done by computer or telephone, students are increasingly starved for the opportunity to sit down with a real live caring professional and talk about "sex, lies, and career development." The need for quality human interaction seems palpable.

IMPERATIVE 5. *We must forge cooperative relationships with faculty, advising professionals, other student affairs professionals, administrators, and student groups to take advantage of the "multiplier effect" that such cooperative relationships can have in furthering our goal of enhanced student career development.*

Recent estimates suggest that more than 77 percent of freshmen and sophomores are uncertain of their choice of major, while 82 percent have little actual experience in the academic fields that they are considering. More than 50 percent of students change their majors at least once before they graduate, some as many as five or six times (Pennsylvania State University, 1990, p. 3). As I suggest in Chapter One, many students feel trapped into making inappropriate "vocationally oriented" career choices because of increasing economic pressure. These and other social and economic forces require that colleges and universities reevaluate the linkage between academic advising and career counseling.

Acknowledging a trend among faculty of abandoning past commitments to academic advising, many colleges and universities have established an entirely nonfaculty class of professionals to provide undergraduate academic advising. Unfortunately, many of these individuals have little or no background in career counseling or career development. As this group of new professionals continues to seek a professional identity, we as career services professionals must embrace and enlist them in our mission of career development. Only through a structural merger between academic advising and career counseling will it be possible to bring the necessary resources to bear on the ever-increasing and complicated career development needs of students in the 1990s. Similarly, cooperative, mutually supportive alliances with faculty, other student affairs professionals, and students will spell relief for overburdened career center professionals in the years ahead.

IMPERATIVE 6. *We must redouble our efforts to meet the changing career development needs of an increasingly diverse student body.*

In their chapter on career counseling, Heppner and Johnston identify attention to the increasing multicultural diversity of the student body as a major theme, and they provide ten solid suggestions to help the career professional respond to that increasing diversity. In her chapter on career programming, Yerian has suggested that much of the innovative programming now being done by career centers has been developed in response to the unique needs of various special interest groups. Demand for such special career programming will certainly increase as the diversity of the student body continues to reflect the changing demographics of the nation, and we as career professionals must position ourselves to meet those demands. To assist the career professional, Yerian has included in the appendix to her chapter a list of contact information from more than one hundred institutions where innovative programs have been implemented, many of them in the interest of better meeting the career development needs of diverse populations.

One fascinating fact about innovations designed to meet the unique needs of special interest groups is that such innovations invariably also enhance our ability to meet the needs of the majority as well. By redoubling our efforts to meet the changing career development needs of the increasingly diverse student body, we are likely to improve the quality of our services to everyone.

IMPERATIVE 7. *We must accept our position as the most obvious and continuing link between corporate America and the academy, but we also must maintain our focus on career development and not allow ourselves to be seduced into institutional fundraising at the expense of quality career services.*

The sometimes uncomfortable coupling of career services with the development function is likely to intensify in the years ahead. As fiscal constraints become ever more severe, institutions of higher education will increasingly be forced to look to private sources to supplement their operating budgets. As the one continuing link between higher education and the corporate world, there will be intense pressure for career center staff to become more involved in the development function. We must accept this challenge of involvement without being swallowed up by the development office, which does not share our history of commitment to student services. The trick will be to share our contacts and knowledge of the corporate culture to enhance institutional development without compromising our commitment and focus on student career development.

IMPERATIVE 8. *We must acknowledge and accept that on-campus recruiting as we have known it is a thing of the past and develop alternative means of facilitating the transition from college to work.*

It seems certain that the social and economic forces that I describe in Chapter One and that Stewart discusses in Chapter Three will bring an end to on-campus recruitment as we know it. The fact that most of the Fortune 1000 companies are decreasing in size, together with the fact that most of the expected employment growth in the foreseeable future will be in small companies, virtually dictates our need to redefine placement. Much of this volume speaks to this task of redefinition.

IMPERATIVE 9. *We must resolve the ambiguities that exist about our role in delivering alumni career services and solicit from our alumni associations the resource support necessary to provide those services.*

The 1990s will see continued and mounting pressure for colleges and universities to provide career services to alumni. The ongoing downsizing and restructuring of U.S. business suggest that the days when a college graduate secured employment with a large corporation from graduation until retirement are over. As I point out in Chapter One, more companies are relying on contracting as a means of purchasing professional services. There is very little job security in such a system, meaning that individuals will require career counseling and support throughout their working lives. Many college graduates will naturally look to their alma mater for this assistance and support. Most alumni associates are eager to provide career services, but few have the expertise to do so, fewer still understand the enormous cost of life-span career services, and none seems prepared to provide the resources necessary to establish comprehensive alumni career services. In one way or another, most colleges and universities will need to address this issue in the 1990s.

IMPERATIVE 10. *We must advocate more effectively for resources to maintain and increase our role in facilitating student career development within the academy, and we must become more efficient and innovative in our use of existing resources.*

It should be a matter of grave concern to the profession that at a time when social, economic, and political forces, as described throughout this volume, are placing ever-increasing demands on career center services, colleges and universities are cutting our budgets. In an era when special interest groups are placing ever greater demands on various student affairs agencies, career services often get short shrift. It is difficult to get our agenda before administrative decision makers because our issues seem rather mundane compared to hate crimes, rising suicide rates, eating disorders, AIDS education and prevention, and general crisis intervention. We simply cannot sit back and allow a service so vitally important to the core mission of the academy to be decimated by budget cuts.

Each of the individual chapter authors acknowledges and recognizes the importance of advocacy in maintaining and expanding the resource base that will be necessary if career centers are to remain viable institutions in the 1990s. On this issue, a call to action, as advocated by Heppner and Johnston, seems particularly warranted. Perhaps a wake-up call for faculty and administration on this issue is also appropriate. As career services professionals, we must do a better job of educating faculty, administrators, and employers about the centrality of our services to the mission of the academy. In recognition of this centrality, a small number of institutions have recently realigned career services administratively so that they now report to the chief academic officer of the institution rather than to the chief student services officer. Such a move may or may not be beneficial to our cause, but one thing is certain: we are in a struggle for survival.

Outside the academy, our struggle for survival requires a more aggressive effort from our professional associations to develop political clout for the purpose of supporting and influencing national and state legislation that affects career development and career education. The ineffectiveness of our professional associations in this arena is not surprising given our ambiguous and unfocused professional identity. We must devote more energy to both issues.

But in addition to stepping up our role as advocates, we must also learn to do more with less, or at least do as much with less. The innovative use of staff, as advocated by Heppner and Johnston, and the implementation of innovative programs, such as those described by Yerian, will be instrumental in helping us achieve this goal, as will the judicious use of technology, as suggested by Stewart. The borrowing of proven marketing and service delivery techniques from business and industry, as suggested by Heppner and Johnston, also seems eminently sensible. Similarly, much of what we do lends itself to the recent trend toward the variously named quality management techniques that are now being applied with considerable success within higher education (Miller, 1991). The *Handbook for College and University Career Centers* (Herr, Rayman, and Garis, in press) is one attempt to assist career services professionals in the task of better managing their resources. Finally, despite all efforts to avoid it, the 1990s have brought a new era of fees-for-service. Beg, borrow, or steal, the future of the career services profession is at a crossroads, and it is a time for advocacy.

## References

Council for the Advancement of Standards for Student Services and Development Programs (CAS). *CAS Standards and Guidelines for Student Services and Development Programs.* Washington, D.C.: CAS, 1986.

DeShong, R. L., Davis, D. L., Peterson, M. B., and Rayman, J. R. "Video Interviewing: An Effective Alternative for the Multi-Campus School?" *Journal of Career Planning and Employment,* 1990, *50* (3), 23–25.

Herr, E. L., Rayman, J. R., and Garis, J. W. *Handbook for College and University Career Centers.* Westport, Conn.: Greenwood, in press.

Miller, R. I. (ed.). *Adapting the Deming Method to Higher Education.* Washington, D.C.: College and University Personnel Association, 1991.

Pennsylvania State University. *Division of Undergraduate Studies Report.* Unpublished manuscript, Division of Undergraduate Studies, Pennsylvania State University, 1990.

Rayman, J. R. "Computers and Career Counseling." In W. B. Walsh and S. H. Osipow (eds.), *Career Counseling: Contemporary Topics in Vocational Psychology.* Hillsdale, N.J.: Erlbaum, 1990.

*JACK R. RAYMAN is director of career development and placement services and affiliate professor of counseling psychology and education at The Pennsylvania State University, University Park.*

# INDEX

Accountability, career services, 34
Admission assistance, 27–28
Advising: faculty, 25–26, 104; preprofessional, 25–26, 30
Alumni career services: and career centers' role, 17; career programming, 89–91
Alumni placement services: job notification systems, 50; on-campus interview-ing service, 50–51; range/categories, 48; resources, 49; résumé service, 49
American Association of Engineering Societies, 4
American University, 91, 93
Americans with Disabilities Act of 1992, 38, 84
Andrews, S., 68
Arizona State University, 49, 82
Assessment: and bias/stereotyping, 71; computer-administered/-interpreted, 102; diagnostic, instruments, 68–69; and individual needs, 66–68; services summary, 20
Association of American Colleges, 86
Astin, A., 8
Astin, H., 8
Axelrod, S., 8

Barnard, C., 85
Bechtel, D. S., 30, 31, 33
Belcher, J. O., 80
Belenky, M. F., 65–66
Benezel, L. T., 24]
Bhaerman, R. D., 80
Bluefield State College (W. Va.), 81–82
Blumenfeld, W. J., 88
Bolles, R. N., 17
Bordin, E. S., 8
Borow, H., 14
Bowdoin College (Brunswick, Maine), 89
Breneman, D. W., 39
Brooks, L., 71
Brown, D., 71
Buhler, C., 66
Burney, D. A., 85
Businesses: manufacturing-/service-based shift, 4–5; professional/scientific employment, 6; restructuring/global competition, 4; small, increase, 5–6. *See also* Defense industry; Employers

Cage, M. C., 7
Cam Report, 4, 5, 6
Cannon, D., 81
Career assistance practitioners: associations, 27; backgrounds, 26; functions, 27. *See also* Staff
Career Beliefs Inventory, 68
Career centers: and alumni career services, 17; atmosphere, 59–60; design, 59–60; and client developmental needs, 65–66; and economic recession, 4, 38; fiscal constraints, 7; and global competition, 4; and job market information, 15; and manufacturing- vs. service-based economy, 4–5; mission, 58–59; 1980s boom, 3–4, 37; peer staffing, 61–63; philosophical/psychological bases, 63–64; and process knowledge/skill, 16–17; and professional/scientific employment practices, 6; professional staffing, 60–61; program evaluation, 94–95; program prioritization/promotion, 59; services summary, 18–20; and small-company market, 5–6; socioeconomic influences, 4–7; and specialized education/training, 17; and student debt, 6; and student diversity, 6–7, 70–74, 104–105; theoretical paradigm, 7–8; and total quality management, 94. *See also* Career services
Career choice predictors, 14
Career choice reality therapy, 5
Career counseling: as authority, 73; and bias, 71, 73–74; and decision-making skills, 16; evolution, 25; importance, 103–104; low priority, 57; offices, 25; research and practice, 74–76; services summary, 18; and student diversity, 70–74; underutilization, 71
Career development: and career services, 105; cycle models, 95; and decision-making skills, 16; defined, 8; and human development, 8; importance;

Career development (continued)
10–11, 33–34; individual responsibility for, 6; and job-seeking/-getting skills, 16–17; lifelong nature, 101; life-span model, 8–10; and multicultural diversity, 71–72; paradigm, 11–17; and placement services, 46–47; and self-knowledge, 11–14; and work world knowledge, 14–16
Career information: delivery systems, 15–16; services summary, 19–20
Career Life Assessment Skills Series, 89
Career programming: alumni, 89–91; context evaluation, 80; employee, 89; and experiential learning, 91–93; and focus groups, 81; gay/lesbian/bisexual students, 87–88; international students, 91; majority students, 81–83; minority students, 85–87; models, 95–98; and needs assessment, 79–81; persons with disabilities, 84–85; returning adult students, 88–89; special populations, 83–91; and student career expectations, 5; and student needs, 80–81
Career services: accountability, 34; and admissions assistance, 27–28; alumni, 17; assessment/research summary, 20; and career counseling/planning, 27; and career development, 105; centralized, 28–30; collegial/coordinated, 32–33; communications summary, 20; and constituent-specific career programs, 28; and cooperative education/internship programs, 26; and counseling offices, 25; decentralized, 30–31; describing, 24; and faculty advising, 25–26; and faculty relationships, 104; financial resources, 106–107; imperatives, 101–107; importance, 33–34; information support summary, 19–20; institutional importance, 33–34; and institutional needs, 28; and job search assistance, 27–28; minority students, 25; and placement services, 24–15, 58; placement summary, 18–19; planning/counseling summary, 18; and preprofessional advising, 25–26, 30; professional identity, 103; programming summary, 19; role, 106; satellite, 32; and student diversity, 6–7, 70–74, 104–105; and

students/families, 33; and technology, 101–103; training summary, 20. See also Career centers
Career Transitions Inventory, 68
Carey, R., 16
Carnegie Commission on Higher Education, 28, 30
Case Western Reserve University, 85
Casella, D. A., 4, 82
Chapman, W., 11
Charleston Southern University, 86
Clemson University (S.C.), 91, 93
Clinchy, B. M., 65–66
Cold War, 5
College of William and Mary (Williamsburg, Va.), 92
College Placement Council (CPC), 8, 24, 25, 26, 29, 40, 44, 92, 95
College Recruitment Database, 44, 55
Commission on Professionals in Science and Technology, 4, 39
Communication services summary, 20
Computers: and assessment, 102; and career guidance, 102; and credentials process, 45; and interview scheduling, 42–43; and student résumé system, 44. See also Software; Technology
Constituent-specific career programs, 28
Cooperative education/internship programs, 26, 47–48
Cornell University, 92
Corporations. See Businesses
Council for the Advancement of Standards for Student Services and Development Programs (CAS), 79, 94, 103
Counseling. See Career counseling
Credentials services: electronic storage/retrieval/transmission of, 102; placement office, 44–46
Crites, J. O., 8
Croft, D., 84
Curtin, B. M., 89

Daiger, D. C., 68
Data Sheet Interchange Standard (DASIS), 44, 55
Davis, D. L., 102
DeBroff, S. M., 93
Debt, student, 6
Defense industry, 3, 5
DeShong, R. L., 102
DISCOVER, 81

Dudley, G. A., 8
Dugan, K., 67, 75

Economy: and business restructuring/
global competition, 4; and Cold War
end, 5; and defense industry, 3, 5;
manufacturing- vs. service-based, 4–
5; 1980s boom, 3–4, 37; 1990s recession, 4, 38; and professional/scientific
employment practices, 6; and small-
company growth, 5–6
Education: cooperative/internship, 26,
47–48; experiential, 73; specialized, 17
Elhurst College (Ill.), 90, 92
Employee-job matching systems, 43–44
Employers: and career development services, 46–47; and employee-job matching systems, 43–44; interviewing on
campus, 41–43; needs, 41; student access to, 40–41; targeting of schools by,
40; traditional, groups, 40. See also
Businesses; On-campus recruiting
Erikson, E. H., 66
Experiential learning: and career programming, 91–93; and self-efficacy, 73.
See also Education; Internship programs

Faculty: advisers, 25–26; career assis-
tance role, 27; career services relation-
ship, 104
Figler, H. E., 17, 25, 33, 34
Fitzgerald, L. S., 8
Fitzpatrick, E. B., 28, 32
Focus groups, 81
Fretz, B., 67
Fuqua, D. R., 67, 68

Garis, J. W., 107
Gast, L. K., 29
Gay/lesbian/bisexual (GLB) students,
87–88
Gayellow Pages: The National Edition, 88
Gelatt, H. B., 16
George Washington University, 93
Georgia Institute of Technology, 50
Ginn, A. J., Jr., 25, 32, 34
Ginsburg, S. W., 8
Ginzberg, E., 8
Goldberger, N. R., 65–66
Gordin, E. E., 25
Gottfredson, L. S., 8, 13

Gould, R. L., 66
Graduate Résumé Accumulation and
Distribution, 43
Greenberg, R., 30

Ham, T., 67, 75
Hansen, R. N., 62, 63
Hartman, B. W., 67, 68
Harvard University, 92
Haskell, P., 89
Havinghurst, R. J., 66
Heatley, R., 90
Hecklinger, F. J., 89
Helms, J. E., 71
Heppner, M. J., 68
Heppner, P. P., 57, 67, 74, 75, 76
Herma, J., 8
Herr, E. L., 107
Hispanic Association of Colleges and
Universities, 86
Holland, J. L., 8, 64, 68, 75
Honeck, J., 85
Hope Scale, 69
Hoppock, R., 25
Hotchkiss, L., 14
Hradsky, R. D., 88
Human Resources Information Network,
44, 55
Hurley, J., 85

IBM Employment Solutions, 54
IBM National Support Center for Persons
with Disabilities, 85
Illinois State University, 85
Indiana University–Purdue University
(Indianapolis), 92
Information. See Career information
Interest inventories, 13
Internship programs: and career services,
26; computerized, data base, 92; and
placement services, 47–48
Interviewing. See Job interviewing

Jackson, T., 17
Jacksonville University, 91
Job interviewing: alumni, 50–51; ethical
issues, 72–73. See also On-campus recruiting
Job market: and business majors, 3; and
business restructuring/global competition, 4, 37; and defense industry, 3,
5; information and career centers, 15;

Job market *(continued)*
    and 1990s recession, 4, 38; service-based, 4–5; and small-company growth, 5–6; variety, 14
Job notification systems, 50
Job search assistance, 27–28
Johnson, C. A., 25, 33, 34
Johnson, M. C., 63
Johnston, J. A., 62
Jones, S. L., 87
Jung, C. G., 66
Just-in-time hiring, 6, 54

Kaplan, R. K., 84
Katz, M., 11, 16
Keierleber, D. L., 89
kiNexus, 44, 55
Kirts, D. K., 27, 30, 32, 33, 38
Kivligham, D. M., 76
Knowledge: process, 16–17; self, 11–14; work world, 14–16
Korshgen, A. J., 94
Krumboltz, J. D., 8, 68, 69
Kuder Preference Inventory, 13

Larson, L., 67, 75
Levinson, D. J., 66
Libraries. *See* Placement services: library material
Lopez, F. F., 68

McAuliffe, G. T., 68
McCarty, A., 85
Mason, B., 90
Massarik, F., 66
Michigan State University, 33, 91
Midwest College Placement Association, 44, 45
Miles, J. H., 25
Miller, R. I., 108
Minority student services, 25
Minority students: and bias, 72, 73–74; career programming, 85–87; career services, 25; outreach services, 73; use of term, 85
Mueller, K. H., 24
Murray, N., 85
My Vocational Situation, 68

Nachmann, B., 8
National Association of College and University Business Officers (NACUBO), 39
National Career Development Associa-

tion Professional Standards Committee, 82
Neff, W. S., 8
Neugarten, B. L., 66
New Mexico State University at Carlsbad, 89
Norris, L., 11
North Carolina State University, 52
Norwich University (Northfield, Vt.), 82, 90

O'Hara, R. P., 16
Ohio State University (OSU), 31, 82, 89
On-campus recruiting: alumni, 50–51; and computerized systems, 44; decline, 105–106; and employee-job matching systems, 43–44; and employer groups, 40; and interview scheduling, 41–43; 1980s boom, 3–4; 1990s bust, 4; targeted, 40; third-party, 53–54. *See also* Job interviewing
OPTIONS, 81
Ottinger, C., 5

Paquette, J. W., 45
Paraprofessionals, 62–63
Parham, T. A., 71
Parsons, F., 8, 66
Pennsylvania State University, 3, 90, 104
Perry, W. G., 65, 66
Persons with disabilities, career services, 84–85
Peterson, M. B., 102
Peterson's Connexion, 44, 55
Placement services: alumni, 48–51; and career development, 46–47; and career services, 58; credential service, 44–46; defined, 37–40; and employer access, 40–41; employee-job matching systems, 43–44; government interest in, 39; and interview scheduling, 41–43; job notification service, 50; library material, 51–53; measurement in, 39; résumé service, 43–44, 49; role changes, 24–25; summary, 18–19; and third-party recruiters, 53–54; use of term, 25, 40
Posluszny, S. B., 82
Powell, C. R., 17, 27, 30, 32, 33, 38
Power, P. G., 68
Preprofessional advising, 25–26, 30
Program evaluation, career programming services, 94–95

Psychology: developmental, 65–66; and student abilities/needs, 63; theory and practice, 64; vocational, 66–67
Purdue University, 49, 50, 53

Rabby, R., 84
Racial/ethnic minorities. *See* Minority students
Raimy, V. C., 74
Rayman, J. R., 102, 103, 107
Raymond, D., 88
Recruitment. *See* On-campus recruiting
Résumé services: alumni, 49; software, 44, 55
Returning adult students, 88–89
Ringling School of Art and Design (Sarasota, Fla.), 93
Rivier College (Nashua, N.H.), 82
Roe, A., 8
Rounds, D., 94
Rutgers University, 87

Saint John's College (Annapolis, Md.), 83
Saint Mary's University School of Law (San Antonio, Tex.), 83
Saint Norbert College (De Pere, Wis.), 83
Salomone, P. R., 67–68, 75
San Diego State University, 90
San Francisco State University, 50
Sanford, N., 66
Schlossberg, N.K.C., 8
Scott, G. J., 24, 25, 26, 27, 28, 32, 33, 34
Segal, S. J., 8
Self-Directed Search, 13
Self-knowledge: and ability, 13; and interests, 13; and motivation, 14; and values, 11–13
Seton Hall University (South Orange, N.J.), 86, 90
Sheehy, G., 66
Shingelton, J. D., 28, 32
Shinkfield, A. J., 80
SIGI PLUS, 81
Simon Fraser University (B.C., Canada), 90
Simpkins, K. L., 84
Skills: decision-making, 16; job-seeking/-getting, 16–17
Smith, E. J., 72
Snyder, C. R., 69
Software: career systems, 81; résumé, 43–44, 55. *See also* Computers

Southern Illinois University at Carbondale (SIU-C), 29–30
Staff: career center, 60–63; peer, 61–63; professional, 60–61; training, 63, 69–70. *See also* Career assistance practitioners; Paraprofessionals
Stanford University, 85
State University of New York at Binghamton, 88, 93
State University of New York at Buffalo, 83
Stephens, E. W., 25, 27
Stephens College, 93
Stevens Institute of Technology (Hoboken, N.J.), 85
Stewart, T. A., 87
Strong Interest Inventory, 13
Students: acculturation, 74; assessment of, 67–68; and career programming, 80–81; career expectations, 5, 37, 39; and career services, 33; debt burden, 6; developmental levels, 65–66; gay/lesbian, 87–88; international, 91; multicultural diversity, 6–7, 70–74, 104–105; psychological needs, 63; résumés, 44; returning adult, 88–89. *See also* Minority students
Stufflebeam, D. L., 80
Sue, D., 71, 73, 74
Sundal-Hansen, L. S., 89
Super, D. E., 8, 10, 72

Tarule, J. M., 65–66
Technology, and career services, 101–103. *See also* Computers
Temple University, 87, 89
Testing. *See* Assessment
Third-party recruiters, 53–54
Tiedeman, D. V., 8, 16
Total quality management (TQM), 94
Towson State University (Md.), 84
Training: service summary, 20; specialized, 17; staff, 63, 69–70

University of Alabama, 82, 90
University of Bristol (R.I.), 89
University of California at San Diego, 85
University of Illinois (Urbana-Champaign), 82, 91, 92
University of Minnesota, 92
University of Missouri (Columbia), 62
University of Nevada at Reno, 89, 93
University of North Carolina, 87

University of Northern Iowa, 84, 93
University of Pennsylvania, 88, 89
University of Pittsburgh, 81, 87, 90
University of Portland, 89
University of Texas at Austin, 86, 91
University of the Arts (Philadelphia), 83
University of the South (Sewanee, Tenn.), 82
University of Virginia, 50, 92
University of Wisconsin at LaCrosse, 92
University of Wisconsin at Stout, 94
U.S. Department of Labor, 5, 6, 14, 15, 85

Valliant, G. E., 66
Values: career-related, 11–13; and life, 11–13
Varenhorst, B., 16

Virginia Polytechnic Institute and State University, 86, 91
VitaQuick, 44
Voice mail, 102

Wambrod, C. P., 80
Wampold, B. E., 76
Washington and Lee University, 90, 93
Washington University, 82
Wellesley College, 83, 93
West Chester University (Pa.), 94
Western College Placement Association and California State University, Long Beach, 84
Wiener, N., 89
Winthrop University (Rock Hill, S.C.), 82, 93
*Workforce 2000 Executive Summary*, 6

# Ordering Information

New Directions for Student Services is a series of paperback books that offers guidelines and programs for aiding students in their total development—emotional, social, and physical, as well as intellectual. Books in the series are published quarterly in Spring, Summer, Fall, and Winter, and are available for purchase by subscription and individually.

Subscriptions for 1993 cost $45.00 for individuals (a savings of 33 percent over single-copy prices) and $60.00 for institutions, agencies, and libraries. Please do not send institutional checks for personal subscriptions. Standing orders are accepted.

Single copies cost $14.95 when payment accompanies order. (California, New Jersey, New York, and Washington, D.C., residents please include appropriate sales tax.) Billed orders will be charged postage and handling.

Discounts for quantity orders are available. Please write to the address below for information.

All orders must include either the name of an individual or an official purchase order number. Please submit your order as follows:
   *Subscriptions:* specify series and year subscription is to begin
   *Single copies:* include individual title code (such as SS1)

Mail all orders to:
   Jossey-Bass Publishers
   350 Sansome Street
   San Francisco, California 94104

For single-copy sales outside of the United States contact:
   Maxwell Macmillan International Publishing Group
   866 Third Avenue
   New York, New York 10022

For subscription sales outside of the United States contact: any international subscription agency or Jossey-Bass directly.

OTHER TITLES AVAILABLE IN THE
NEW DIRECTIONS FOR STUDENT SERVICES SERIES
Margaret J. Barr, Editor-in-Chief
M. Lee Upcraft, Associate Editor

SS61 Identifying and Implementing the Essential Values of the Profession, Robert B. Young
SS60 Enhancing the Multicultural Campus Environment: A Cultural Brokering Approach, Frances K. Stage, Kathleen Manning
SS59 Rights, Freedoms, and Responsibilities of Students, William A. Bryan, Richard H. Mullendore
SS58 The College Union in the Year 2000, Terrence E. Milani, J. William Johnston
SS57 Effective AIDS Education on Campus, Richard P. Keeling
SS56 Racism on Campus: Confronting Racial Bias Through Peer Interventions, Jon C. Dalton
SS55 Managing the Political Dimension of Student Affairs, Paul L. Moore
SS54 Dealing with Students from Dysfunctional Families, Robert I. Witchel
SS53 Using Professional Standards in Student Affairs, William A. Bryan, Roger B. Winston, Jr., Theodore K. Miller
SS52 Affirmative Action on Campus, Joseph G. Ponterotto, Diane E. Lewis, Robin Bullington
SS51 Evolving Theoretical Perspectives on Students, Leila V. Moore
SS50 Community Service as Values Education, Cecilia I. Delve, Suzanné D. Mintz, Greig M. Stewart
SS49 Crisis Intervention and Prevention, Harold L. Pruett, Vivian B. Brown
SS48 Designing Campus Activities to Foster a Sense of Community, Dennis C. Roberts
SS47 Responding to Violence on Campus, Jan M. Sherrill, Dorothy G. Siege
SS45 Dealing with the Behavioral and Psychological Problems of Students, Ursula Delworth
SS44 Empowering Women: Leadership Development Strategies on Campus, Mary Ann Danowitz Sagaria
SS41 Managing Student Affairs Effectively, M. Lee Upcraft, Margaret J. Barr
SS39 Enhancing Campus Judicial Systems, Robert Caruso, Will W. Travelstead
SS38 Responding to the Needs of Today's Minority Students, Doris J. Wright
SS37 Expanding Opportunities for Professional Education, Leila V. Moore, Robert B. Young
SS36 Guiding the Development of Foreign Students, K Richard Pyle
SS34 Developing Campus Recreation and Wellness Programs, Fred Leafgren
SS33 Enhancing Relationships with the Student Press, John H. Schuh
SS32 Working with the Parents of College Students, Robert D. Cohen
SS30 Applied Ethics in Student Services, Harry J. Canon, Robert D. Brown
SS23 Understanding Student Affairs Organizations, George D. Kuh
SS22 Student Affairs and the Law, Margaret J. Barr
SS20 Measuring Student Development, Gary R. Hanson
SS4 Applying New Developmental Findings, Lee Knefelkamp, Carole Widick, Clyde A. Parker